New Perspectives in Behavioral & Health Sciences

New Perspectives in Behavioral & Health Sciences is a series of high-quality, compact volumes focused on presenting interdisciplinary perspectives on key, developing, or new topics in Behavioral and Health Sciences. This SpringerBrief series will be of interest to a broad range of researchers and practitioners working in related fields of Behavioral and Health Sciences such as Psychology, Mental Health, Criminology, Public Health, and Social Work.

Suchismita Satapathy ·
Arturo Realyvásquez Vargas · Meghana Mishra

Occupational Health Safety Factors and Their Impact on the Mental Health of Workers

Springer

Suchismita Satapathy
School of Mechanical Engineering
KIIT University
Bhubaneswar, Odisha, India

Meghana Mishra
School of Commerce and Economics
KIIT University
Bhubaneswar, Odisha, India

Arturo Realyvásquez Vargas
Departamento de Ingeniería Industria
Instituto Tecnologico de Tijuana
Tijuana, Baja California, Mexico

Tecnológico Nacional de México
Mexico City, Mexico

ISSN 2731-9296 ISSN 2731-930X (electronic)
New Perspectives in Behavioral & Health Sciences
ISBN 978-981-99-7618-8 ISBN 978-981-99-7619-5 (eBook)
https://doi.org/10.1007/978-981-99-7619-5

This Springer imprint is published by the registered company Springer Nature Singapore Pte Ltd.
The registered company address is: 152 Beach Road, #21-01/04 Gateway East, Singapore 189721, Singapore

Preface

This book includes eight chapters, which focus on the physical, psychological, and mental stress of people suffering from different kinds of job practices. Occupational health and safety (OHS) in the workplace is a debated topic all over the world. Every industry claims that, for the benefit of employees, the organization has its own insurance, casual leave, sick leave system, allowances offered during mid-break. Still, many people are suffering from physical and mental disorders due to work pressure, continuous work, repetitive work, noisy and dusty unhealthy work atmosphere, etc. The discomfort in the workplace is directly proportional to work-related productivity and the performance of employee. In most of the labour-intensive sectors, like the mining sector, construction sector, and agricultural sector, the main cause of hazards, discomfort and MSDs are improper workplace design, which leads to most of the occupational accidents and also impacts on the mental health of workers. Some comfortable indoor white-collar jobs are less strenuous physically, but highly stressful mentally. Long working hours, no family or sociable time, work pressures, continuous sitting or standing postures, competitive atmosphere in the workplace, etc. make people mentally and physically sick.

A number of factors adversely affect the workers by reducing their productivity, such as compelling efforts, repetitive tasks, static and awkward postures, and utilization of inappropriate tools and equipment. The discomfort workplace, work culture, and heavy workload create great impact on the physical health of workers. This discomfort, musculoskeletal disorder and physical sickness, and long working hours also highly impact on the mental health of workers. Besides these factors, wages and gender violence are also important factors for women workers in the workplace. It is estimated that 264 million people go through mental health issues. Depression and anxiety are the prime drivers of physical disorder and vice versa. A recent study by "WHO" estimates that mental disorders cost the global economy US$ one trillion each year in lost productivity and quality. Working environment, type of work, and physical stress in work might be the causes of physical and mental health problems, which has negative effects like harmful use of substances or alcohol, absenteeism, and lost productivity. Workplaces that help people with mental health issue are more likely to decrease absenteeism and increase productiveness and profit. Mental health issues are the major cause of disease and disability worldwide. Many of the disability and sufferings found worldwide are due to mental health problems. So the cause of mental health interventions should be prevented or identified from early stage and need moral support and rehabilitation.

Any workplace can be described as healthy one, where all type of workers actively impart to the organization by following safety rules and protecting their health. Although there are so many risk factors for mental wellness in the working environment, among them the most risk factors are the type of physical stress a workers face during working procedures. Both mental and physical health care are important to keep and sustain workers in the working environment happily. So work type and physical workload must be studied to find relation on mental health of workers. Innovation technology and advancement in automation which can resolve OHS problems can reduce the percentage of accident and reduce work-related fatigue by improving the work system. IoT and AI can trace the failure or accident by warning and can provide comfort reducing repetitive manual work. Automation can easily the tough and lengthy procedures in the workplace and improve productivity in the workplace. Hazard work, contact with harmful chemicals, toughest workplace, which are very difficult and risky place for human health, can be done with the help of robotics technology. Protective and innovative equipment with IoT can save human from dangerous working place and protect their life from risky workplace. This book explores discomfort in working environment and its impact on mental health of varying workplace and some innovative solutions to provide comfort, safety and sustainability in workplace to reduce mental workload. Some employment (e.g. first responders and humanitarian workers) may have a larger personal risk than others, which can have an influence on mental health and be a source of symptoms of mental disorders, as well as lead to harmful use of alcohol or psychoactive drugs. In circumstances where there is a lack of team cohesion or social support, risk may be raised. This book may provide a solution or a helping hand to increase awareness of mental health and wellness among researchers or readers.

Hence, in Chap. 1 discusses in detail about workplace hazards and safety factors, and sustainable measures were suggested to reduce workplace hazards in the workplace. Chapter 2 gives a clear concept on hazards by literature review. Chapters 3 and 4 provide a pictorial representation of the labour-intensive agriculture, construction, and mining sector with clearly describing their hazards and psychological impact on workers' health. Chapter 5 focuses on physical and mental health of animal farmers mental issue detail. Chapter 6 describes the psychological stress of white-collar employees, Chap. 7 explores the agricultural women physical and psychological stress. At the end, Chap. 8 concludes with a comparative analysis of psychological stress scales by implementing on same sample workforce. It is an excellent guide for academicians, research scholars for postulating more innovative practices, framing policies designing devices for extreme comfort of workers or employees.

Bhubaneswar, India — Suchismita Satapathy
Tijuana/Mexico City, Mexico — Arturo Realyvásquez Vargas
Bhubaneswar, India — Meghana Mishra

About This Book

This book examines the occupational health and safety factors in different types of organization by Ergonomic analysis. Psychological factors are also taken into consideration for measuring mental stress of workers, those were physically stressed due to heavy or repetitive work and discomfort at work place. Hazard and risk assessment is also done for employees of labour intensive sectors and white collar employees. Some case studies were taken for farming and animal farming sectors and mental stress are examined by psychological stress scales.

- This book will explain work place discomfort
- The relation between mental health and physical work load
- Gender and type of work performed
- Comparison of mental pressure and type of work performed
- Ergonomics analysis
- Computational analysis
- Safety, sustainability and risk assessment.

Contents

About the Authors

Suchismita Satapathy is an associate professor in the School of Mechanical Sciences, KIIT University, Bhubaneswar, India. She has published more than 130 articles in national and international journals and conferences. She has also published many books and e-books for academic and research purposes. Her areas of interest include production operation management, operation research, acoustics, sustainability, and supply chain management. She has filled three Indian patents, among them two published. She has more than 15 years of teaching and research experience. She has guided many Ph.D. (three completed, three ongoing), M.Tech. (20), and B.Tech. (49) students. Suchismita has published books such as *Production Operation Management* (Stadium Press) and *MCDM Methods for Waste Management* with CRC Press, *Innovation, Technology, and Knowledge Management* with Springer, *Soft Computing and Optimization Techniques for Sustainable Agriculture* by De Gruyter, *The PDCA Cycle for Industrial Improvement, Applied Case Studies* by Springer, and many of her projects are ongoing.

ORCID: https://orcid.org/0000-0002-4805-1793
Scopus Author ID: 55085975400

Arturo Realyvásquez Vargas is a full-time professor from the Department of Industrial Engineering at Tecnológico Nacional de Mexico/Instituto Tecnológico de Tijuana in Mexico. He received a master's degree in Industrial Engineering and a Ph.D. in Engineering Sciences from the Autonomous University of Ciudad Juarez in Mexico. Currently, he is studying a Ph.D. in Innovation in Product Engineering and Industrial Process at the University of La Rioja (Spain). In addition, his main research areas are related to the optimization of industrial processes, lean manufacturing, and ergonomics. He is an active member of the Society of Ergonomists of Mexico Civil Association (Sociedad de Ergonomistas de México, SEMAC) and the Network of Optimization of Industrial Processes (Red de Optimización de Procesos Industriales, ROPRIN). Currently, Dr. Realyvásquez is a National Researcher recognized by the National Council of Science and Technology of Mexico (CONACYT) as level I. Furthermore, Dr. Realyvásquez is an author/coauthor in around 12 papers published in journals indexed in the Journal Citation Reports. He has attended international conferences and congress in Mexico and the USA. Nowadays, Dr. Realyvásquez has supervised more than 20 bachelor theses and five master theses. In addition, Dr. Realyvásquez is the author of one book published by the international publisher Springer, related to ergonomics. Also, Dr. Realyvásquez has edited two IGI Global books, all related to ergonomics.

ORCID: https://orcid.org/0000-0003-2825-2595
Scopus Author ID: 56167726800

Meghana Mishra is a research scholar in the School of Commerce in KIIT University, Bhubaneswar, India. She has published more than six articles in national and international journals, conferences, and book chapters. Her areas of interest include production operation management, economic study of agrisector, sustainability, business process reengineering, ergonomics, etc.

Abbreviations

AI	Artificial intelligence
ANFIS	Adaptive neural-fuzzy inference system
CCTV	Closed-circuit television
DASS	Depression anxiety stress scale
FA	Factor analysis
FAO	Food and agricultural organizations
HoQ	House of quality
ILO	International labour organization
IoT	Internet of things
MCDM	Multicriteria decision-making
MSDs	Musculoskeletal disorders
OHS	Occupational health and safety
OSHA	Occupational safety and health administration
OWAS	Ovako working posture analysing system
PSS	Perceived stress scale
QEC	Quick exposure check
QFD	Quality function deployment
REBA	Rapid entire body assessment
RULA	Rapid upper limb assessment
SWARA	Step-wise weight assessment ratio analysis
WASPAS	Weighted aggregate sum and product assessment
WRMSDs	Work-related musculoskeletal disorders

List of Figures

List of Tables

Chapter 1
Workplace Hazards

Abstract Negative effects, such an increase in mental workload, difficulty focusing, and physical health problems, can result from stress. Due to psychological stress that affects farmers' mental health and productivity, musculoskeletal discomforts and disorders might lead to major health issues. Sometimes employees become uneasy working in unsanitary environments, such as dairy farms. The present study was built on a thorough examination of the literature and a review of publications that focused on the mental strain and workload of framers. It showed that farming is a stressful occupation because of the money, weather, labour overload, social interaction, and agricultural difficulties are main causes of workplace hazard. Similar to farmers, construction site workers' physiological factors are impacted by their hard workload, and evidence suggests that their substantial mental workload is to blame for their high levels of stress.

Keywords Workplace hazard · Physical health · Mental workload · Physiological factors · Workload

1.1 Introduction

Risks at work emerge when the surroundings can lead to illness, injury, or even death. Equipment, toxic materials, unsafe working practises, and human behaviour are just some of the numerous facets of the workplace that might pose risks. Sometimes risks or hazards in the workplace occur unknowingly, and sometimes due to a lack of mind. Hazards like slips, trips, and falls; operating dangerous machinery; and electrical hazards are very common in an organization. The workers have a habit of drinking alcohol or drugs out of habit and also face accidents. Sickness, sleeplessness, mental illness, or careless activities may be the main causes of accidents among many workers in industries, construction sites, or mining areas. But an untrained and unskilled worker often faces accidents in ignorance of safety regulations. When working in dangerous conditions, both workers and employees must be vigilant. Proper testing of alcoholism, drug addiction, and the health and mental condition of

S. Satapathy et al., *Occupational Health Safety Factors and Their Impact on the Mental Health of Workers*, New Perspectives in Behavioral & Health Sciences,
https://doi.org/10.1007/978-981-99-7619-5_1

the worker must be done, and safety tools must be provided to them. These small steps can prevent hazards and ensure the safety of workers.

1.2 Workplace Hazards and Causes

Workplace hazards occur due to a lack of safety in the workplace. It may occur due to machines, the environment, or a lack of precautions and awareness. In almost all kinds of jobs, risk factors are associated with them. Hazards may be classified into seven types: environmental like environmental hazard, biological hazards, chemical hazards, ergonomic hazards, physical hazards, safety hazards, psychological hazards, etc. Sometimes, mental hazards were due to lack of security at work, lack of job satisfaction, monetary matters, personal or family conflicts, etc. Physical hazards are sometimes accidental, unexpected, and sudden. Both physical and psychological hazards impact the work life, performance of the person, and quality and productivity of work delivery. Blue-collar workers in the industrial and construction sectors have to work on machines and equipment. They have to perform weightlifting and repetitive work, and their workplace is also not that organized. Even their work is more physical and continuous, lasting more than 7–8 h. Lack of work allowance, rest allowance, continuous night shift work, pressure of job change, variation in wage rate, etc. also affect the mental stress of workers in blue-collar jobs. Sometimes, family disturbances, conflicts in the workplace, consumption of alcohol or any other drugs, and sickness are the causes of mental stress and physical hazards. Carelessness in the workplace or uncertain hazards may also cause accidents in the workplace. Purple-collar job holders usually perform some jobs in the office and some in the field. The physical risk of field jobs is the same as that of white-collar job holders, but during an official job, they have to sit in one position and work repetitively for a long time. White-collar workers usually perform indoor jobs in a constant posture, so they may face muscle pain, eye strain, repetitive motion injuries, etc. The workplace air quality is not proper, and due to a lack of physical work and exercise, they face lifestyle diseases. Work performance for women is a balance between their household work, and office or workplace. performance of women farmers in agrisector is heavy and repetitive in nature (Ma. Elena, 2009) compared to others. Hence, work performance and safety also vary as per gender. The performance of an elderly person cannot be similar to a young person. An elderly person may be slow at doing some jobs but may be experienced at doing them perfectly. But, hazards never distinguish between experienced work, slow work, and speed work. Hence, safety precautions are the only measure to avoid hazards.

Those who work in fish farms and agribusiness may suffer from fungal infections, skin infections, etc. Even mining workers suffer from pulmonary diseases and skin cancer. Workplaces full of dust, gas, and chemicals make people sick with lung cancer. Workers engaged in heavy and repetitive work suffer from MSDS and backbone pain. Long working hours, sitting, and mental jobs cause less physical stress but more mental strain and ergonomic disorders. Sudden accidents, collisions, falling from stairs, etc. are unexpected disorders that are the cause of workplace hazards. Workplace hazards can be stopped by modifying and organizing the workplace. With the use of modern personal protective equipment, workplace disorders can be restricted.

1.3 Safety Factors in the Workplace

To prevent hazards or risks, safety plays a vital role in the workplace. People like to do their jobs happily in an injury- and accident-free environment. Safe, accident-free industrial equipment and machines not only improve the productivity of the organization, but they also provide a safer and better working environment for workers. Organizations provide protective equipment for their employees' safety, like helmets, boots, gloves, proper clothes, and oxygen masks when required. Night shift duties with a one-day break, allowances for rest, food, medical, and insurance, proper holidays and breaks, proper medical checkups, training, education, flexibility in the workplace, etc. make employees comfortable and more productive. From time to time, safety training, rewards, and recognition make workers comfortable in their work environment. With these factors, proper care must be taken with the help of IoT and AI devices to put alarm systems, beeps, proper electricity, and fire systems in place to avoid hazards. Environmental factors like humidity, noise, temperature, and a proper lighting system make the work environment more comfortable for long-hour workers. When people work in their flexibility and comfort zone, they can work for a long time and face no MSDs. Hence, safety factors are more important in a workplace and must be taken care of through study and scientific analysis.

1.4 Sustainability Measures

Sustainability measures for workplace safety mean designing or modifying the workplace for the comfort of workers working in that system. It can be done by following safety guidelines. But sustainable measures mean providing safety by considering three factors: environmental, social, and economic. Environmental safety can be achieved in the workplace by making it pollution-free. By minimizing waste materials, recycling them, and storing hazardous materials in a proper way, the environment can be made pollution-free. Dust, poisonous gases, and chemicals must be properly taken care of. Proper guidelines and policies must be planned and followed to make ecological systems safe and non-hazardous. Economic costs include costs due to damage to equipment, machines, etc. The cost also includes the cost of the loss of life of employees and medical costs due to injuries suffered due to hazards. Hence, to avoid economic losses, regular maintenance, insurance, and hazard-detecting devices must be implanted, and protective equipment must be provided to all employees. Reporting unsafe conditions in the workplace, planting trees, practising correct working posture, reducing workplace conflicts, and taking social measures to reduce stress can be helpful to maintain sustainability in the workplace. Regular safety programmes and safety training make the work environment safe and improve the social security of employees.

1.5 Research Questions

In view of the workplace safety and hazards, the hazards of workers are different depending on the type of work, process of work, and the physical and mental condition of the worker who is performing the work. Particularly the system or the workplace where the job is done is also important. Even environmental conditions, the temperature, and humidity of the workplace are also impacts on the work efficiency. Even the machines used their noise, and vibration also affects working environment.

Hence, it becomes necessary to understand the actual key risks affecting the workers' physical and mental health condition and their relation with hazards around the globe. Moreover, more priority-based research needs to be done with regard to the safety issues (McIntyre et al., 2009). Although there is much research found on mental illness and physical discomfort of workers, no research is found which can methodologically show how it is impacting on workplace safety. This kind of research will show a guideline to researchers regarding workplace discomfort and mental ill health conditions.

The main objectives of this work were:

(a) Describing agricultural work-related stresses and its outcomes as mental sickness for farmers all over the world; (b) highlighting the white-collar workers' mental stress; and (c) showing the discomfort in the construction and mining sector and their psychological stress; (d) discussing the intervention strategies for gender- and work-type psychological stress.

To successfully achieve the objectives of this work, the below research questions were developed.

- What are the discomforts and stress achieved by agricultural community?
- How does work burdens effect on the mental health conditions of women farmers?
- What safety practices have been considered in the construction and mining sectors and their effect on psychological stress?
- How psychological stress varies with gender and profession?

1.6 Important Points

Sustainability and safety factors have a complex relationship between each other. Both are equally important for the well-being of the human race. These two factors provide environmental, social, and economic factors in every organization and occupational health and mental wellness to employees. It will also provide an insight into modifying the workplace for the comfort of workers. Ultimately, healthy and happy workers will perform better and the organization will grow. The farmers and workers remain unhealthy mentally or physically; their efficiency will be reduced, which will affect the productivity. The sick worker will be mentally disturbed and may face accidents or hazards. Hence, some studies in both developing and developed countries have disclosed that they are experiencing worsened psychological health disruption, which has prompted policymakers to consider how best to address different risk actors.

References

Ma. Elena, C.-J. (2009). Health consequences of rural women's productive role in agriculture in the Philippines and other developing countries. *Journal of International Women's Studies, 10*(4), 95–110. Available at http://vc.bridgew.edu/jiws/vol10/iss4/7

McIntyre, B., Herren, H., Wakhungu, J., & Watson, R. (2009). *Agriculture at a crossroads: International assessment of agricultural knowledge.*

Chapter 2
Literature Review on Mental Health and Workplace Hazards

Abstract When people attempt varied levels of complex activities, mental stress has a significant impact on how well they succeed. Higher mental stress levels seem unpleasant for humans to experience, and they may have an impact on their ability to complete activities satisfactorily. Stress at work had an extremely negative emotional and physical impact. It is a risky situation with higher fatality rates than any other occupation with regard to a select few occupations like teaching, administrative work, or office work when people are depressed and unable to handle the stress. In order to analyse the gender differences in the types of work done and the work culture, comparative analysis is crucial so that a judgement about work strain and mental health can be made. In this chapter, a brief literature review is conducted to find the workplace hazards in workplace and its effect on mental stress.

Keywords Workplace hazard · Mental stress · Work strain

2.1 Introduction

Both physical and psychological stress impact human health. A mentally and physically stressed person is not able to perform properly in the workplace. Their social life is also disturbed. Irrespective of gender, age or type of work many people suffer from mental health issues. Physical, psychological, and mental health are interrelated to each other. Mental health issues are an emerging problem in society and an important point of discussion among researchers. Hence, an extensive literature review is essential to discuss mental stress as per, gender, age, and job type. A mentally unstable person usually shows poor work performance and remains socially secluded and economically poor. Their work and social life are both disturbed. This condition prompts them towards alcoholism, smoking, drug addiction, etc. An unstable and disturbed person is also a threat to society. Sometimes depression, stress, and anxiety can make them aggressive and suicidal and ascend into immoral and unethical behaviour. Excruciating physical workload and continuous shift duties make employees highly stressed. Sleepless nights, insufficient breaks and holidays, tyranny

S. Satapathy et al., *Occupational Health Safety Factors and Their Impact on the Mental Health of Workers*, New Perspectives in Behavioral & Health Sciences,
https://doi.org/10.1007/978-981-99-7619-5_2

management, overdemanding work goals, etc. pressurize workers. Workplace harassment, work hazards, and highly risky jobs are the enhancers or drivers of mental illness. It is the enabler of depression, anxiety, stress, and trauma. Sometimes mental sickness led to the workforce being disturbed and causes workplace hazards. Both are interrelated, and their effects are dangerous for human, society, and the organizations.

2.2 Literature Review About Workplace Hazards

Workplace hazards are the main cause of injuries and accidents in the workplace, where the mortality rate is very high. People do different kinds of jobs all over the world, and the injury and hazard rate varies from job to job. Some jobs are hazardous and prone to accidents while some are non-physical yet onerous in nature, but mental stress is very high. Some jobs are field jobs and are done in difficult working conditions and adverse incident-prone environment. As jobs are conditional and different from each other, safety rules are also different to save human lives and develop a risk-free work environment. The hazards in the mining and construction sectors are not similar to those in farming, industries, or office jobs. Workplace hazards also depend on the frequency of jobs performed, the kind of exposure to work, and the degree of exposure. The job of firefighters is very risky because it involves saving resources and people's lives. They have to risk their lives. DeJoy et al. (2017) have explained that in the USA, the firefighter death rate is higher than that of most other workers. Eastlake et al. (2015) has explained that firefighters can be exposed to 120-decibel noise and suffer from cardiovascular disorders. Similarly, traffic police, forest guards, policemen, and army personnel, although are well trained to perform their duties continuously for long hours, have direct exposure to climate change. Still, many of them suffer a lot from discomfort from their job. Brown et al. (1998) and Cho et al. (2014) have discovered lower-back, shoulder, waist, neck, wrist, and leg pain in police officers. Satapathy et al. (2009), Fiaz et al. (2018), Prajapati et al. (2015), and Satish et al. (2015) have reported leg, neck, knee, lumbar joint, and lower-back pain in traffic police due to continuous standing. Tavares Neto et al. (2013) and dos Santos et al. (2014) have observed lower-back pain and discomfort in army officers. Hazards on construction sites may occur due to slips, trips, falls, or falls of materials, electricity, machinery, noise at the workplace, or hazards due to repetitive work. Shirur and Torgal (2014) have explained that a huge number of hazards or accidents take place at construction sites. Construction workers are not the only victims of accidents; the public, including children, is also affected. Kumar and Bansal (2013) have written that the decreasing number of workers occurs due to accidents, which reduces the image of the construction industry. Koehn and Datta (2003) have explained the importance of safety rules and regulations, which will help issues like poor quality work and unsafe working conditions and also improve the productivity sector. The mining sector is full of hazards. The environmental conditions are very poor in the mining sector. High humidity, high temperatures, and a risky environment are not suitable for human health. Miners also face work-related hazards inside mines. Cho and Lee (1978) have explained that mining hazards include accidents at work, diseases due to dust, noise pollution, etc. Patterson and Shappell (2010) have found that mining accidents are due to errors performed by the operators, irrespective of the type of mine. Zheng et al. have used FAHP to assess accidents in a hot and humid environment. Have revealed that factors such as noise, heat, vibrations, and other harmful climatic conditions adversely affect the health of farmers. Crimes and Enticott (2019) have analysed the social and psychological impacts of the farmer's subjective well-being and their tendency to work when suffering mental health problems. Ngai and Pissarides (2007) have explained that the transformation of agriculture occurs with an increase in agricultural income and productivity.

2.3 Literature Reviews on Sustainability and Safety in the Workplace

Sustainable organizations must keep the proper balance between profits, human resources, and the environment. Without protecting the welfare and safety of human resources, the organization or industry cannot survive in long run. Sustainability takes care of social safety, profit in the economy, and environmental safety conditions that can be achieved in an organization. But without occupational health and safety for the workers, sustainability cannot be completely achieved in an organization. Occupational safety accidents and hazards will have a great impact on the economy and reputation of an organization. Niven (2002) discussed wellness and safety investments and risk control methods. Tompa et al. (2006) explained that economic interventions are essential for the workplace health and safety of industries. Lamm et al. (2007) found a relationship between workplace safety and firm productivity. Cagno et al. (2013) explored workplace safety and small- and medium-sized businesses. Accidents and hazards will create a fear factor in society, which in turn leads the reputation of the company or organization into ruins, which will automatically have a severe impact on the economy. Environmentally unsuitable organizations will make people unhealthy, so organizations must provide a safe atmosphere, protective equipment and tools for the well-being and safety of workers.

2.4 Conclusion

To achieve security in an organization, safety guidelines and rules must be recorded and adhered. To avoid hazards or accidents, mandatory fire safety, electricity safety, and other safety training must be provided to the employees. CCTV cameras must be installed in accident-prone areas, and danger symbol placards must be placed in those areas properly noticeable. During work, protective helmets, gloves, boots, glasses, etc. must be provided as work equipment for the respective job. To keep the workers' health in good condition and to provide a sustainable environment, proper systems must be used when dust, poisonous gases, or harmful chemicals are dealt with. When all the organizations follow environmental and safety guidelines properly and stakeholders of the organization, management, and governments take immediate actions concerning the safety and sustainability of both inside and outside systems, the occupational safety of workers could be guaranteed hundred percent.

References

Brown, J. J., Wells, G. A., Trottier, A. J., Bonneau, J., & Ferris, B. (1998). Back pain in a large Canadian police force. *Spine, 23*(7), 821–827.

Cagno, E., Micheli, G. J. L., Masi, D., & Jacinto, C. (2013). Economic evaluation of OSH and its way to SMEs: A constructive review. *Safety Science, 53*, 134–152.

Cho, K. S., & Lee, S. H. (1978). Occupational health hazards of mine workers. *Bulletin of the World Health Organization, 56*(2), 205.

Cho, T. S., Jeon, W. J., Lee, J. G., Seok, J. M., & Cho, J. H. (2014). Factorsaffecting the musculoskeletal symptoms of koreanpolice officers. *Journal of Physical Therapy Science, 26*(6), 925–930.

Crimes, D., & Enticott, G. (2019). Assessing the social and psychological impacts of endemic animal disease amongst farmers. *Frontiers in Veterinary Science, 6*, 342.

DeJoy, M., Smith, T. D., & Dyal, M. A. (2017). Safety climate and firefighting: Focus group results. *Journal of Safety Research, 62*, 107–116.

dos Santos, M. C., Krueger, E., & Neves, E. B. (2014). *XXIV Congresso Brasileiro de Engenharia Biomédica;* Universidade Federal de Uberlândia, SBEB; 2014. Out. Distribuição anatômica das queixas álgicas de policiais militares do Paraná 2014.

Eastlake, A. C., Knipper, B. S., He, X., Alexander, B. M., & Davis, K. G. (2015). Lifestyle and safety practices of firefighters and their relation to cardiovascular risk factors. *Work, 50*, 285–294

Fiaz, M. W., Ahmad, A. A., Munawar, A., Rabia, K., & Fatina, M. (2018). Prevalence of musculoskeletal pain in trafficpolice wardens of Lahore, Pakistan. *Rawal Medical Journal, 4*(1), 61–63.

Koehn, E. E., & Datta, N. K. (2003). Quality, environmental, and health and safety management systems for construction engineering. *Journal of Construction Engineering and Management, 129*(5), 562–569.

Kumar, S., & Bansal, V. K. (2013). Construction safety knowledge for practitioners in the construction industry. *Journal of Frontiers in Construction Engineering, 2*(2), 34–42.

Lamm, F., Massey, C., & Perry, M. (2007). Is there a link between workplace health and safety and firm performance and productivity? *New Zealand Journal of Employment Relations, 32*(1), 72–86.

Ngai, R., & Pissarides, C. (2007). Structural change in a multi-sector model of growth. *The American Economic Review, 97*(1), 429–443.

Niven, K. J. M. (2002). A review of the application of health economics to health and safety in healthcare. *Health Policy, 61*, 291–304.

Patterson, J. M., & Shappell, S. A. (2010). Operator error and system deficiencies: Analysis of 508 mining incidents and accidents from Queensland, Australia using HFACS. *Accident Analysis and Prevention, 42*(4), 1379–1385.

Prajapati, P., Modi, K., Rahul, K., & Shah, A. (2015). A study related to effect of job experience on health of traffic police personnel of Ahmedabad City, Gujarat, India. *International Journal of Interdisciplinary and Multidisciplinary Studies (IJIMS), 2*(6), 127–133.

Satapathy, D. M., Behera, T. R., & Tripathy, R. M. (2009). Health Status of Traffic Police Personnel in Brahmapur City. *Indian Journal of Community Medicine, 34*(1), 71–72.

Satish, S., Phadke, D., Revati, R., & Iqbal, R. (2015). Work related musculoskeletal symptoms among traffic police: Cross sectional survey using Nordic musculoskeletal questionnaire. *International Journal Recent Research Interdisciplinary Science, 04*(2), 26.

Shirur, S., & Torgal, S. (2014). Enhancing safety and health management techniques in Indian construction industry. *International Journal of Engineering and Technical Research, 2*(4), 52–56.

Tavares Neto, A., Faleiro, T. B., Moreira, F. D., Jambeiro, J. S., & Schulz, R. S. (2013). Lombalgia na atividade policial militar: análise de prevalência, repercussões laborativas e custo indireto. *Revista Baiana de Saúde Pública, 37*(2), 365–374.

Tompa, E., Dolinschi, R., & de Oliveira, C. (2006). Practice and potential of economic evaluation of workplace-based interventions for occupational health and safety. *Journal of Occupational Rehabilitation, 16*, 375–400.

Chapter 3
Ranking and Prediction of Sustainability and Safety in Agrisector with Analysing Physical Workload and Its Impact on Mental Workload

Abstract This chapter deals with farmers working long hours using hefty, sharp tools in harsh weather and adverse climatic conditions. In this unsafe and unhealthy atmosphere, farmers become unsocial and depressed. Due to stress, farmers experience musculoskeletal dysfunction and other health issues. The lives of agrifarmers have become more stressful due to the growing use of automation technology, manure and fertilizer use, and mechanized innovations. Non-organic products, higher costs for agricultural products, and new, complex legislation make farmers' lives more stressful. The unpleasant working environment and heavy, repetitive work of farmers increased the mental workload and physical pain simultaneously. So in this section, a study is conducted to find factors impacting sustainability and safety in agriculture. Then physical load is analysed with ergonomics, and its impact on mental health is studied by relating the physical stressors with psychological stressors.

Keywords Agriculture · Musculoskeletal disorders · Ergonomic · Posture analysis · Farming · Mental stress

3.1 Introduction

Agriculture, or farming, is a traditional job done by farmers with or without the help of cattle. Small-scale or nominal farmers have less land to use to conduct this job manually, and large-scale farmers use bullock carts, modern farming equipment, and tractors. Farming is an essential but dangerous occupation. A farmer has to work day and night in an agrifield in hot summers and heavy rain. Farmers face a lot of health issues during work due to the adverse climate. Farming equipment is the main cause of cuts, scratches, and injuries for farmers. The farmer has to work on sand and muddy ground with bare feet, so many kinds of insect bites and fungal infections are common for them. Dust, sunshine, sunny, and humid climates are the main causes of skin infections for farmers. Different types of farming are done, so farming jobs are not seasonal; it is a continuous job. A farmer has to perform different types of farming operations, like sowing, seeding, ploughing, transplanting, watering,

S. Satapathy et al., *Occupational Health Safety Factors and Their Impact on the Mental Health of Workers*, New Perspectives in Behavioral & Health Sciences,
https://doi.org/10.1007/978-981-99-7619-5_3

fertilizer spraying, weeding, land preparation, harvesting, etc. Sometimes, loading, unloading, ploughing, etc. are also done by farmers. All farming operations need hard labour and repetition. Heavy workloads and repetitive work create musculoskeletal disorders, muscle pain, and back pain symptoms among farmers. The noise of a tractor and agrimachines, the smell of diesel, and the dusty atmosphere are also not healthy for farmers. The use of machines and tractors makes the agricultural process smooth, but the noise and vibration generated are bad for the farmer's health. Lack of safety in using tools and machines and repetitive work in agriculture with constant posture create musculoskeletal disorders among farmers. Hence, in this chapter, an effort is made to find the challenges of sustainability and safety in the agriculture sector by analysing physical workload. The heavy workload in the farming sector creates physical discomfort, body pain, and back pain, which affects productivity, and the farmer is under great mental pressure. The farmer suffers from psychological problems like depression, anxiety, and stress. Hence, in this chapter, the mental health of the farmer is predicted by analysing the physical workload. Table 3.1 shows the challenges of sustainability and safety factors in farming operations.

3.2 Ergonomic Analysis in Farming

To reduce physical stress and mental stress during farming, workplace safety must be taken care of. Proper design of the workplace and advances in farming equipment may help to reduce work pressure up to a certain level. When the workplace is comfortable and healthy, the farmer can work comfortably and its work performance will also improve. Farmer has to work in agrifields in hot summer and heavy rain. Adverse climatic conditions reduce the capacity/performance of farmers. Farmers have to use traditional tools, tractors for their farming operations. These tools cause injury and are the main cause of accidents. The noise and vibrations in tractors are also beyond human audible range. Dust, pesticides, etc. are hazards and also create pulmonary diseases and breathing discomfort. Many times, farmers are sick due to snake/insect bites and fungal infections during their farming operation in mud/sand, etc. The most important reason of farmers' discomfort is continuous, repetitive farming operations. Farmers face shoulder, back, leg, and hand pain during farming operations due to discomfort. The uncomfortable working postures are the main cause of musculoskeletal disorder, which needs extensive ergonomic analysis and design modification. By considering ergonomics in designing workplaces and equipment or farming tools, the farmer can save his life and can perform better. With the improvement in ergonomic design of agricultural equipment, safety and workplace comfort can be achieved.

Villarejo and Baron (1999) have discovered that farmers suffer from back pains and shoulder pains, due to vibration in farm machines. Some farmers are unable to continue their farm jobs due to injuries, sprains and strains. Bhattacharyya and Chakrabarti (2012) have done some research on the female workforce occupied in the tea industry in Assam. It was found that the women use baskets for carrying tea leave

Table 3.1 Challenges faced in sustainable and safe farming operation

Agriculture operation	Safety	Sustainability
Land preparation and ploughing	• Tractor overturns and accidents faced • Fall from tractor • Injury from hand tools • Exposure to high heat and humidity • Insect bites	• Loss of soil moisture • Soil erosion • Loss of organic material • Unfavourable biological effect
Seeding	Ergonomic risk to farmer	
Transplantation	Ergonomic risk	
Manure mixing and spreading	• Ergonomic risk • Chemicals are not good for health (skin cancer) • Contaminate vegetables and cause diseases	• Soil quality hampered • Water contamination • Water infiltration and retention • Soil pollution
Weeding	• Injury during using weeding tools • Ergonomics risk to farmers	• Polluting water ways • Harm to birds, mammals, and insects • Damaging native plants
Harvesting	• Injury during using harvesting tools • Ergonomics risk to farmers	• Economic risk
Insecticide spraying	• Ergonomics risk • Insecticides are not good for health, skin, eyes, and lungs	• Air, water, and soil pollution • Crops, plants, birds, animals are affected
Watering	• Ergonomics risk for farmer	• Land degradation • Mismanagement of groundwater
Dehusking	• Ergonomics risk	• Air pollution

on their back, so suffered with musculoskeletal issues and back pains. Hence both the authors had modified the bucket by using anthropometric information which had reduced their body discomfort and back pain. Jatinder and Rana (2012) have found the discomfort in carrying tool during the weeding activities, so the tools were designed by considering anthropometric content. Naeini et al. (2014) wrote that the agriculture sector is a highly dangerous sector/hazardous sector, where farmers suffer from maximum musculoskeletal disorders (MSDs). Nunes (2009) has differentiated three types of hazard factors (i.e. physical factors, psychosocial factors, and individual factors). McAtamney and Corlett (1993) have explained about RULA, REBA and QEC tools for Ergonomic assessment. Ren and Xiao (2009), Sanjog et al. (2012), and have explored the RULA analysis technique for workplace designs. Ren and Xiao (2009) and Sanjog et al. (2012) have the explored an ergonomic assessment for farmers by RULA ergonomic tool. Karhu et al. (1977, 1981) have successfully used "Ovako Working Posture Analysing System (OWAS)" for the steel industry.

3.3 Research Methodology

To study the challenges of sustainability and safety in farming, a set of standard questionnaires is designed with extensive literature review and a survey is conducted by Likert scale (1–5), which are totally agree, agree, no opinion, disagree, totally disagree respectively. To assess the sustainability and safety challenges of farming operations in four developing countries, like "India, Nepal, Bangladesh, and Mexico" survey is carried on. Table 3.2 shows Questionnaire for survey Vandermeer (1992) and Wright et al. (2007). Then factor analysis is conducted by minitab-17 for 22 no of questions on challenges of agrifarming. SWARA (step-wise weight assessment ratio) multicriteria decision-making method is used to prioritize the most important challenge. From the literature analysis, questionnaires and personal interactions with the farmers, and further opinion of decision-making experts (Table 3.3), in this study, the SWARA method was used for calculating the weights, and corresponding ranking of the criterion as well as sub-criteria were done accordingly. The still photos of farmers were initially captured with a digital camera, taking into account the typical poses used during various farming operations. When taking the pictures, care was given to both machine-based and traditional methods of farming. The "ErgoFellow-3.0 software" was then applied, and RULA scores were taken into consideration when making additional recommendations for action levels. A RULA tool was employed to find discomfort posture in farming or risky posture, further OWAS (Ovako working analysis system) was used to do more analysis on physical discomfort. Further, the DASS (Depression, Anxiety, Stress Scale) psychological scale is used to check the impact of physical discomfort on mental stress. ANFIS is used to predict mental stress with MATLAB-17.

3.4 Result and Discussion

Although many research papers are written about injuries in agricultural sectors worldwide, the research is limited to a few. Hamberg-van Reenen et al. (2008) and Patel et al. (2010) have written about injuries due to cutting tools. To find challenges of implementation of sustainability and safety in agrisector minitab 16 is used for statistical analysis. Under the nine dimensions like ergonomic risk, biological risk, chemical risk, physical risk, psychological risk, safety and sustainability risk (i.e. social, economic, and environmental) 21 items are selected from 22 items having Cronbach alpha value of more than 0.5, items below 0.5 is discarded and not used for further analysis. Table 3.4 shows factor analysis result.

Then SWARA is used to prioritize challenges of safety and sustainability in agrisector.

Table 3.2 Questionnaire for survey

Sl. no	Questionnaire	1	2	3	4	5
1.	Risk of insect bites					
2.	Involvement of the private sector in farming is nil					
3.	Fungal infection and bacterial infection in agrifield					
4.	Lack of advanced technology in farming					
5.	Natural calamities and climate change its effect on agrisector					
6.	Lack of training about biodiversity to reduce CO_2 emissions					
7.	Lack of social relationships					
8.	Lack of competitiveness among farmers					
9.	Lack of knowledge about crop rotation and crop cover					
10.	Musculoskeletal problems from repetitive and constant posture work					
11.	Musculoskeletal problems from lifting and carrying tools or equipment					
12.	Injuries from hand tools					
13.	Risk of falling down from a tractor					
14.	Exposure to vibration/noise/smoke of tractors					
15.	Small land and small-scale farmers					
16.	In security of farmers due to loneliness					
17.	Lack of skill/education and knowledge of farmers					
18.	Lack of awareness about integrated and natural pests use					
19.	Large production costs required in farming compared to profit					
20.	Financial problems and low profits in farming					
21.	Fertilizers and pesticides create pollution					
22.	Fall of groundwater level					

Table 3.3 Decision-making experts' characteristics

Area	Qualification	No of experts
Agriculture scientist	Doctoral	1
Medical sector	MBBS	1
Environmental sector	Master degree	1
Irrigation sector	Master degree	1
Academicians	Doctoral	1

3.4.1 SWARA Method is Used to Prioritize Challenges

The SWARA method was applied to define the weights of the criteria and sub-criteria on the basis of following steps:

Table 3.4 Factor analysis

	Item	F1	F2	F3	F4	F5	F6	F7	F8	F9
Environmental Challenges	5, 6, 9	0.814, 0.525, 0.702								
Social challenges	2, 8		− 0.815 − 0.732							
Economic challenges	19, 20			0.664 0.785						
Safety challenges	4, 17				0.668 0.826					
Physical challenge	12, 13					0.844 0.642				
Psychological challenge	7, 16						− 0.625 − 0.826			
Chemical challenges	18, 21							− 0.870		
Ergonomic challenges	10, 11, 14								− 0.517 − 0.855 − 0.555	
Biological challenges	1, 3									0.858 0.500

Stage 1: According to the significance, the parameter is sorted, where the most important is placed first, and the least important is placed last.

Stage 2: The relative significance of average value (s_j) is measured on the basis of the importance of the parameter c_j compared to the criterion $c_j + 1$.

Stage 3: The calculation of coefficients' (k_j) is as below:

$$k_j = \begin{cases} 1 & j = 1 \\ s_j + 1 & j > 1 \end{cases},$$

Stage 4: The calculations of re-calculated weights (q_j) are as below:

$$Q_j = \begin{cases} 1 & j = 1 \\ \frac{q_{j-1}}{k_j} & j > 1 \end{cases}$$

Stage 5: The calculations of comparative weights (w_j) of the evaluation conditions are as below:

$$W_j = \frac{q_j}{\sum_{k=1}^{n} q^k}$$

where n = number of the parameters (Fig. 3.1 and Table 3.5).

After the Swara ranking From Table 3.6, it is found that Ergonomic challenges are the most important challenging factor. So ergonomic analysis is conducted by RULA. Table 3.7 shows RULA score of agrifarming operations like land preparation, winnowing, seeding, etc. Rula score ranking from 1 to 7. It is found that the agrioperations like harvesting, plucking, pesticide spraying score is 7, it means investigation and changes are required soon. Hence for the agrioperations like harvesting, plucking and pesticide spraying more researches are done by OWAS ergonomic tool (Tables 3.8).

3.4.1.1 *OWAS SCORE for Ergonomic/Physical Discomfort Analysis*

To measure mental stress of farmers, depressions, anxieties, and stress levels were measured by the use of DASS-21 parameters scale (Figs. 3.2, 3.3, 3.4 and 3.5).

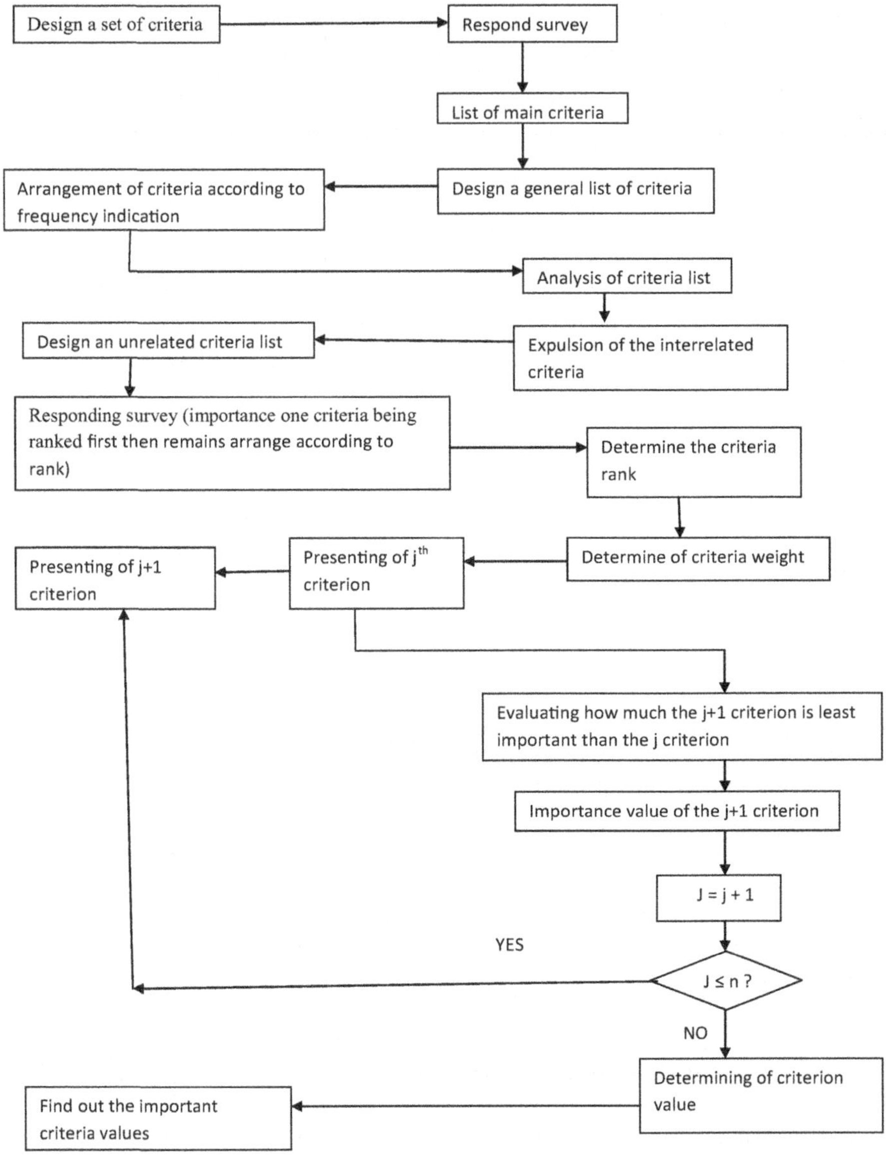

Fig. 3.1 Steps of the SWARA method for measuring parameter weights. *Source* Zolfani (2014)

Table 3.5 Challenges and subchallenges

Challenges/parameters	
C_1	Environmental challenges
$C_{1\text{-}5}$	Natural calamities and climate change its effect on agrisector
$C_{1\text{-}6}$	Lack of training about bio diversity to reduce CO_2 emissions
$C_{1\text{-}9}$	Lack of knowledge about crop rotation and crop cover
C_2	Social challenges
$C_{2\text{-}2}$	Involvement of the private sector in farming is nil
$C_{2\text{-}8}$	Lack of competitiveness among farmers
C_3	Economic challenges
$C_{3\text{-}19}$	Large production costs required in farming compared to profit
$C_{3\text{-}20}$	Financial problems and low profits in farming
C_4	Safety challenges
$C_{4\text{-}4}$	Lack of advanced technology in farming
$C_{4\text{-}17}$	Lack of skill/education and knowledge of farmers
C_5	Physical challenge
$C_{5\text{-}12}$	Injuries from hand tools
$C_{5\text{-}13}$	Risk of falling down from a tractor
C_6	Psychological challenge
$C_{6\text{-}7}$	Lack of social relationships
$C_{6\text{-}16}$	In security of farmers due to loneliness
C_7	Chemical challenges
$C_{7\text{-}18}$	Lack of awareness about integrated and natural pests use
$C_{7\text{-}21}$	Fertilizers and pesticides create pollution
C_8	Ergonomic challenges
$C_{8\text{-}10}$	Musculoskeletal problems from repetitive and constant posture work
$C_{8\text{-}11}$	Musculoskeletal problems from lifting and carrying tools or equipment
$C_{8\text{-}14}$	Exposure to vibration/noise/smoke of tractors
C_9	Biological challenges
$C_{9\text{-}1}$	Risk of insect bites
$C_{9\text{-}3}$	Fungal infection and bacterial infection in agrifield

Table 3.6 Final weight of parameters on environmental challenges

Sub parameter	Relative significance of average value	Coefficients	Recalculated weights	Last weights
$C_{1\text{-}5}$		1	1	0.374888902
$C_{1\text{-}6}$	0.14	1.14	0.877192982	0.328849914
$C_{1\text{-}9}$	0.11	1.11	0.790263948	0.296261184
			2.667456931	

Table 3.7 Overall ranking of parameters along with subparameters is based on categories

Signs	Parameter along with subparameters	Weight values	Overall position
C_1	Environmental challenges	0.1833	2
C_2	Social challenges	0.1553	3
C_3	Economic challenges	0.1351	4
C_4	Safety challenges	0.1354	3
C_5	Physical challenge	0.1021	6
C_6	Psychological challenge	0.1292	5
C_7	Chemical challenges	0.0821	7
C_8	Ergonomic challenges	0.1841	1
C_9	Biological challenges	0.0641	8
$C_{1\text{-}5}$		0.068717136	5
$C_{1\text{-}6}$		0.060278189	8
$C_{1\text{-}9}$		0.054304675	10
$C_{2\text{-}2}$		0.052389202	13
$C_{2\text{-}8}$		0.072910798	3 (3rd)
$C_{3\text{-}19}$		0.069197561	4
$C_{3\text{-}20}$		0.065902439	6
$C_{4\text{-}17}$		0.05293578	12
$C_{4\text{-}4}$		0.06246422	7
$C_{5\text{-}12}$		0.054831481	11
$C_{5\text{-}13}$		0.047268519	15
$C_{6\text{-}16}$		0.043192488	16
$C_{6\text{-}7}$		0.048807512	14
$C_{7\text{-}18}$		0.043004762	17
$C_{7\text{-}21}$		0.039095238	18
$C_{8\text{-}10}$		0.077427195	1 (1st)
$C_{8\text{-}11}$		0.073916137	2 (2nd)
$C_{8\text{-}14}$		0.060441165	9
$C_{9\text{-}1}$		0.03335	19
$C_{9\text{-}3}$		0.02875	20

3.5 Psychological Test

The "Depression, Anxiety, and Stress Scale (DASS-21)" is used to gauge how depressed, anxious, and stressed farmers are when performing specific farm-related duties under challenging weather conditions. The DASS-21 was used by the questioner to assess the discomfort levels and the effect of field discomfort posture on psychological stress levels (Lovibond et al., 1995; Vidyadhara et al., 2020). Table 3.9

Table 3.8 Rula score for farming operation

Activity		RULA score	Proposed actions
Land preparation	Manual land preparation	7	Investigation and changes are required immediately
	Land preparation using a bullock-drawn plough	5	Investigation and changes are required immediately
	Tractor implements for ploughing	4	Further investigation is needed and changes may also be required
Seeding	Direct transplanting	5	Investigation and changes are required immediately
Watering		4	Investigation and changes are required soon
Fertilizing		4	Investigation and changes are required soon
Plucking		7	Investigation and changes are required soon
Pesticide Spraying		5	Investigation and changes are required soon
Weeding	Manual weeding	5	Investigation and changes are required immediately
	Carrying unwanted plants after weeding	4	Further investigation is needed and changes may also be required
Harvesting	Manual harvesting using sickle	7	Investigation and changes are required immediately
	Making bundles of rice stalks	5	Investigation and changes are required immediately
Threshing	Manual threshing by striking on wood	5	Investigation and changes are required immediately
	Threshing by machine	5	Investigation and changes are required soon
	Separating chaffs after threshing	4	Further investigation is needed and changes may also be required
Winnowing		4	Investigation and changes are required soon

shows DASS question used for collecting data, and Table 3.10 shows DASS score of farmers.

Scale, which was formed by questions 1 through 7, is called depression scale, was part of the DASS-21 parameters scale. Its scores were divided into five categories, (i.e. "normal" with scores between 0 and 9; mild depression with scores of 10–13; moderate depression with scores of 14–20; severe depression with scores of 21–27; and extremely severe depression with scores of 28 and more. The Anxiety sub-scale

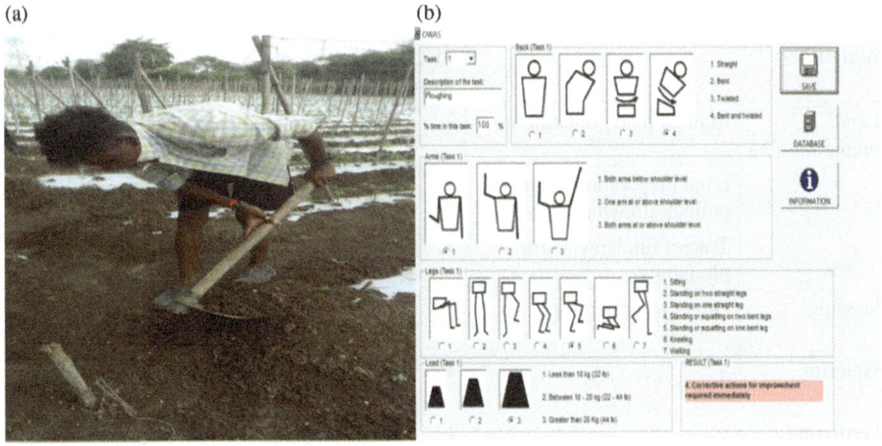

Fig. 3.2 **a, b** Manual ploughing and OWAS score

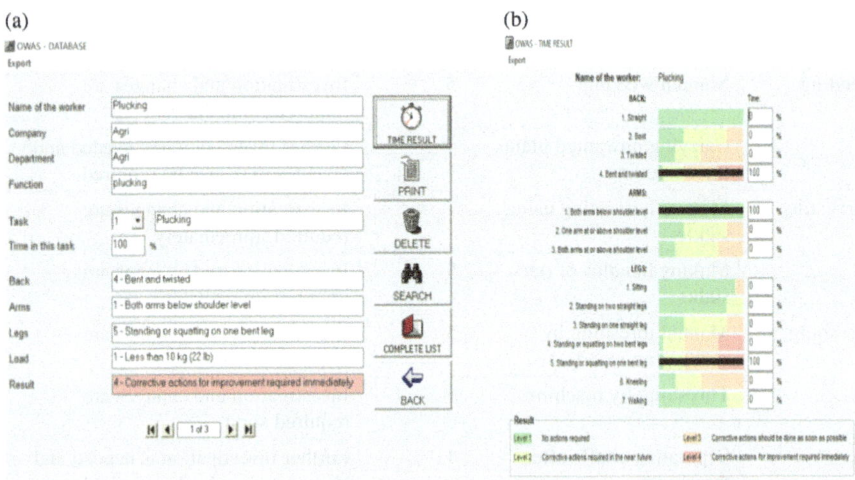

Fig. 3.3 **a, b** Ploughing time scale analysis for ploughing

was comprised of questions 8 through 14, and it was broken down into five categories based on the scores: "normal" with scores of 0–7; mild anxiety with scores of 8–9; moderate anxiety with scores of 10–14; severe anxiety with scores of 15–19; and extremely severe anxiety with scores of 20 and more). The scores for all three categories of depression, anxiety, and stress were then determined by adding up the respondents' scores for the pertinent variables. Farmers' physical and psychological characteristics are measured and show positive relationship with each other. Then internal characteristics, such as calories burned, pulse rate, high blood pressure, low blood pressure, temperature, and oxygen level, are used as inputs against outcomes

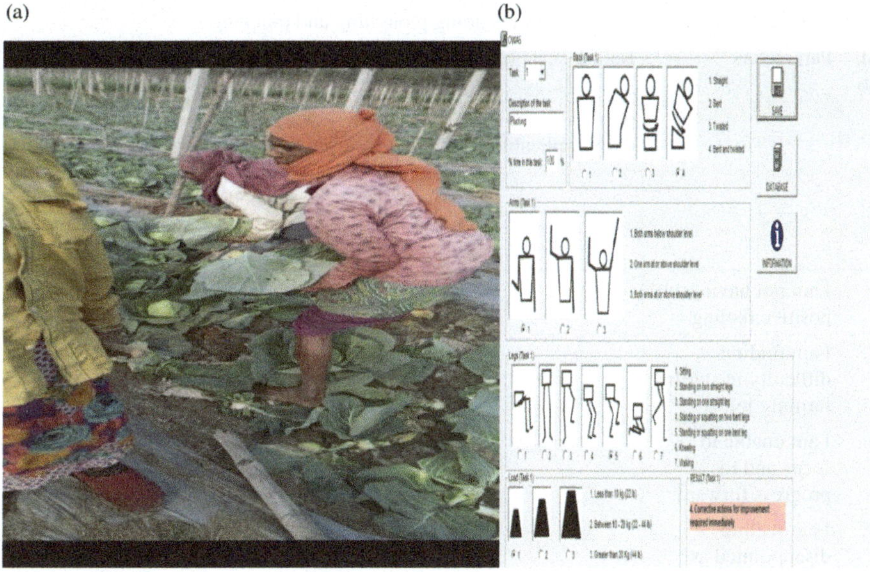

Fig. 3.4 **a**, **b** OWAS score for plucking

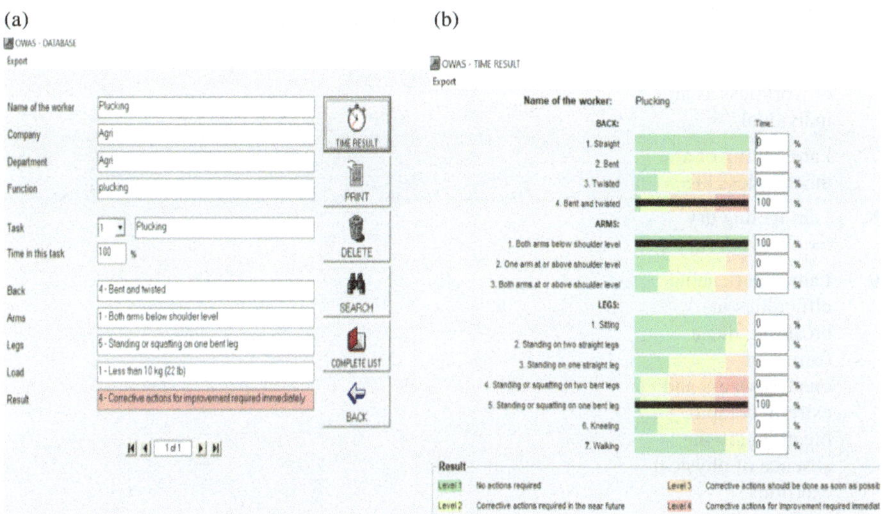

Fig. 3.5 **a**, **b** OWAS results and time score for plucking

Table 3.9 Calculation of DASS for famers doing ploughing and plucking

Sl. no	Parameters	Rating-scale (please put √ mark whichever is applicable)			
		0 (Not-applicable)	1 (Applicable to some-degree)	2 (Applicable to a considerable-degree or a good-part of time)	3 (Applicable to very-much or most of the time)
1.	I am not having any positive feeling			√	
2.	I am finding difficulty in starting farming job		√		
3.	I am unable to focus and to progress forward				√
4.	I am feeling disappointed as well as insecure			√	
5.	I am not feeling excited to work in field				√
6.	I have the feeling of worthless as an individual		√		
7.	I am feeling of a meaningless life				√
8.	I am feeling dry mouth syndrome			√	
9.	I am experiencing difficulties in breathing like a feeling of breathlessness and extremely rapid breathing, in the absence of physical exertions		√		
10.	My hand and body parts are shaking and feeling cold			√	
11.	I am anxious about the situations that is putting me in panic and making me a fool				√

(continued)

Table 3.9 (continued)

Sl. no	Parameters	Rating-scale (please put √ mark whichever is applicable)			
		0 (Not-applicable)	1 (Applicable to some-degree)	2 (Applicable to a considerable-degree or a good-part of time)	3 (Applicable to very-much or most of the time)
12.	I am feeling as if getting nearer to panic		√		
13.	My heartbeat is discontinuous				√
14.	I am feeling scared without any suitable reason			√	
15.	I feel it difficult to wind down				√
16.	I am over-reacting to situations		√		
17.	I am feeling as if utilizing lots of nervous energy			√	
18.	I start myself getting restless				√
19.	I am unable to relax		√		
20.	I am feeling of getting narrow-minded of anything that is keeping me away from my activities				√
21.	I am feeling of becoming sensitive			√	

to predict mental stress in the chosen farmer. A few studies, including those by Trapp et al. (2014), Kanjo et al. (2018), and Russo et al. (2017), have investigated the effects of internal factors on human physical and mental health, including calories burned, pulse rate, high blood pressure, low blood pressure, temperature, and oxygen level. Hence, measurements such as calories burned, pulse rate, high blood pressure, low blood pressure, temperature, and oxygen saturation were taken using the device with the aid of medical professionals and common measuring tools like thermometers, sphygmomanometers, and oxygen meters, among others. Therefore, the ANFIS model in MATLAB 2016 was used to forecast the output (the mental stress of farmers), and the input variables included the number of calories burned, pulse

Table 3.10 DASS-21 score for farmers

Mental Stress	Normal	Mild	Moderate	Severe	Extremely severe
Depression	**0–9**	**10–13**	**14–20**	**21–27**	**≥ 28**
Number of responds (%)	11 (20.75)	116(30.19)	07 (14.56)	11 (21.52)	06 (9.54)
Anxiety	**0–7**	**8–9**	**10–14**	**15–19**	**≥ 20**
Number of farmers responded (%)	14 (24.85)	07 (13.08)	23 (41.22)	05 (15.12)	04 (8.43)
Stress	**0–14**	**15–18**	**19–25**	**26–33**	**≥ 34**
Number of responds (%)	19 (35.17)	07 (12.32)	21 (41.09)	06 (9.89)	02 (3.66)

*n = Total number of farmer

rate, high blood pressure, low blood pressure, temperature, and oxygen saturation, among others.

3.6 Mental Stress Prediction

To find the correlation coefficient for measuring the mental stress of framers few data was collected (i.e. kcal burnt, pulse rate, high BP, low BP, temperature and oxygen level, etc.), by standard device with the help of medical professional.

Out of 53 farmers, numbers of selected female farmers was 23 and the number of selected male farmers was 30. From percentages representation for female farmers (Fig. 3.6), it was found that 6 (26.08) having normal depression, 4 (17.39) having mild depression, 5 (21.73) having moderate depression, 4 (17.39) having severe depression, and 4 (17.39) having extremely severe depression. In anxiety scale 6 (26.08) having normal anxiety, 3 (13.04) having mild anxiety, 9 (39.13) having moderate anxiety, 3 (13.04) having severe anxiety, and 2 (8.69) having extremely severe anxiety. As per stress scale 6 (26.08) having normal stress, 5 (21.73) having mild stress, 7 (30.43) having moderate stress, 3 (13.04) having severe stress, and 2 (8.69) having extremely severe stress.

From percentages representation for male farmers (Fig. 3.7), it was found that farmers that 9 (30.00) having normal depression, 7 (23.33) having mild depression, 5 (16.33) having moderate depression, 5 (16.66) having severe depression, and 4 (13.33) having extremely severe depression. In anxiety scale 10 (33.33) having normal anxiety, 6 (20.00) having mild anxiety, 5 (16.66) having moderate anxiety, 7 (23.33) having severe anxiety, and 2 (6.66) having extremely severe anxiety. As per stress scale 11 (36.66) having normal stress, 4 (13.33) having mild stress, 7 (23.33) having moderate stress, 5 (16.66) having severe stress, and 3 (10.00) having extremely severe stress.

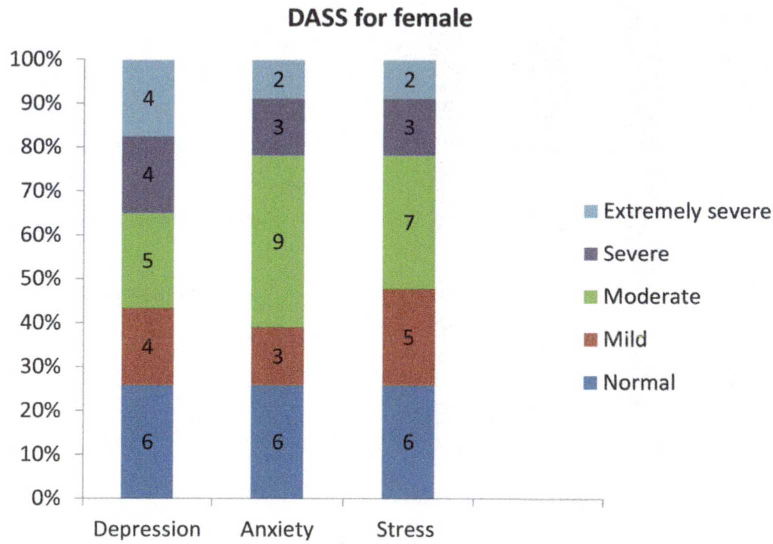

Fig. 3.6 Percentage representation for female farmers

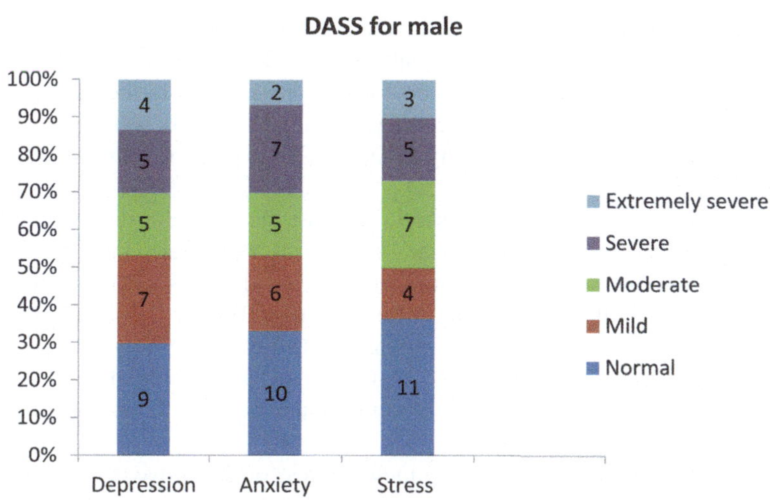

Fig. 3.7 Percentage representation for male farmers

In Fig. 3.8, it was explored that 13 male farmers and 10 female farmers belonged from age between 18 and 25, 9 male farmers and 8 female farmers from age between 26 and 35, 8 male farmers and 5 female farmers from age between 36 and 50 were measured their internal parameter with standard devices.

From Fig. 3.9, frequency of age standardized was measured by DAS. It was found that from age 18 to 25 out of 53 farmers, 17 farmers have depression, 16 farmers have

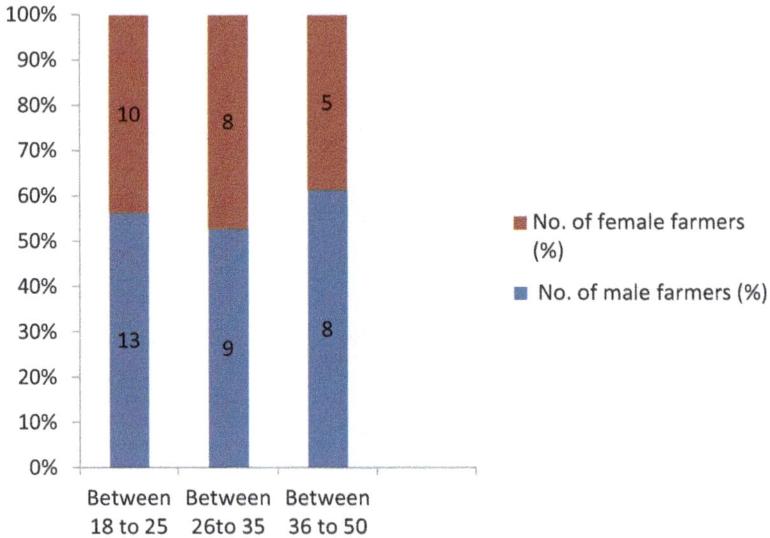

Fig. 3.8 Percentage representation for male and female farmers with age standardized

anxiety and 14 farmers have stress. From age 26–35 out of 53 farmers, 21 farmers having depression, 23 farmers having anxiety, and 27 farmers having stress. From age 36–50 out of 53 farmers, 15 farmers have depression, 14 farmers have anxiety, and 12 farmers have stress. In between age 26 and 35 farmers were suffering with maximum level of depression, anxiety and stress. So to predict mental stress ANFIS model was used.

A linear regression equation is used to forecast the Mental Stress of farmers by taking the internal parameters such as "kcal burnt, pulse rate, high BP, low BP, temperature and oxygen level". Mental stress is considered as a dependent variable and other variables like "kcal burnt, pulse rate, high BP, low BP, temperature, and oxygen level" are called as independent variables.

Mental wellness of Farmers = − 2.77 − 0.0317 kcal − 0.0342 Pulse rate + 0.0181 High Blood pressure + 0.0319 Low blood pressure + 0.205 Temperature − 0.178 Oxygen level.

Then ANFIS is used for predicting mental stress of the above regression model. By MATLAB, where, C_1 = kcal burnt, C_2 = Pulse rate, C_3 = High BP, C_4 = Low BP, C_5 = Temperature and C_6 = Oxygen level.

The bell-shaped membership function with 200 epochs was chosen for the ANFIS network to produce the most efficient model. Figures 3.10 and 3.11 show the mental stress prediction, errors, and ANFIS data for the ANFIS models, respectively. It was found that ANFIS was able to predict farmers "Mental Stress" more accurately and with fewer errors.

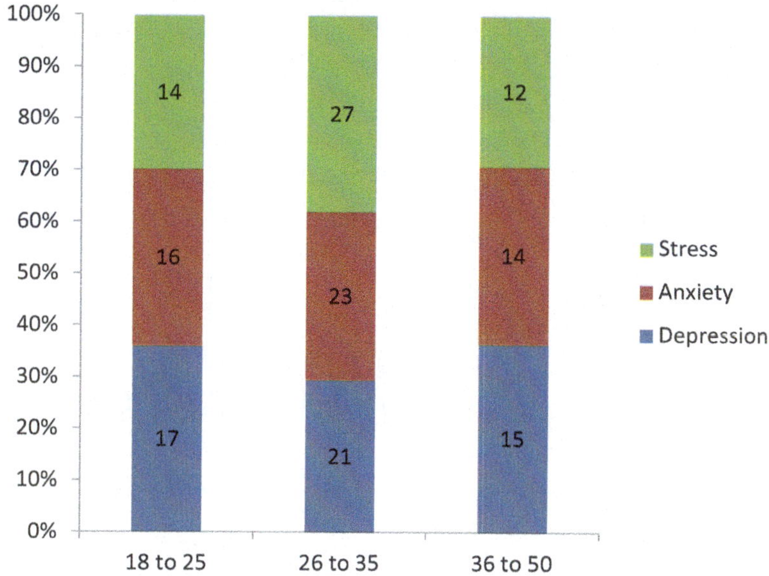

Fig. 3.9 Frequency of age standardized measure DAS in age from 18 to 50

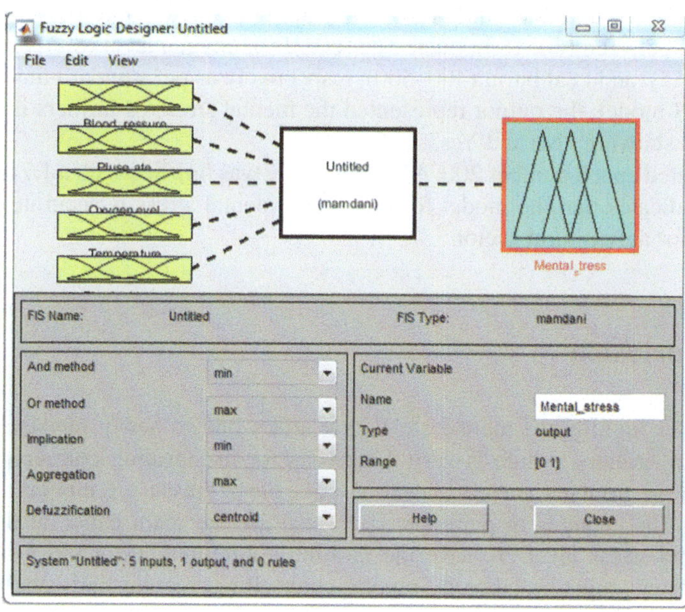

Fig. 3.10 Prediction for mental stress of farmers by ANFIS

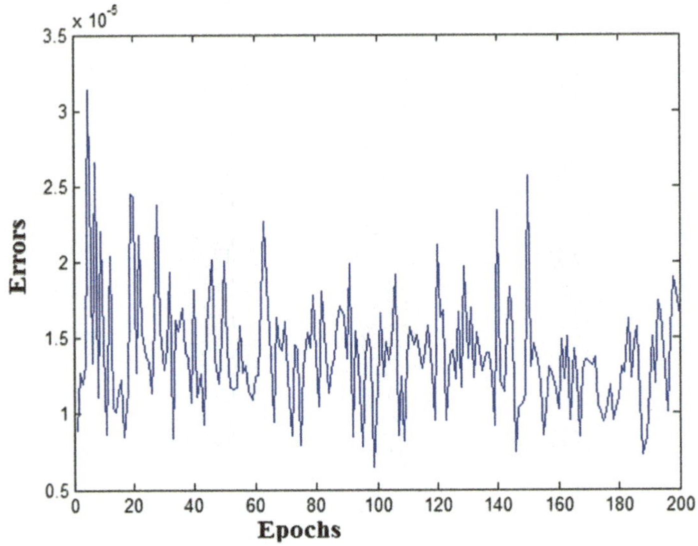

Fig. 3.11 Errors of mental stress prediction of farmers by ANFIS

The minimum and maximum ranges for input parameters like blood pressure is considered between (60–180), pulse rate (60–100), oxygen level (80–100), temperature (20–55), and kcal burnt (400–500), respectively as per standard measurement. For ANFIS model, the output represented the mental stress of farmers in the range of "0 to 1" showing "No and Yes".

At targeted epoch number 200, ANFIS training was finished with a 1.7142261005 error. It indicates that the model for predicting mental stress is accurate and has a low error for agricultural sector.

3.7 Conclusion

This chapter highlighted mental stress that arises due to heavy physical stress of agricultural farmers, which is very dangerous for the farming community, and it changes the internal parameters of the body, like blood pressure, temperature, oxygen level, etc. The changes in parameters are also are the main cause of depression, anxiety, and stress level. To save the farming community from this kind of risk, necessary steps must be taken by regular counselling, regular body checkups, etc. Advanced agricultural_machines can be developed to be operated without human interventions and can reduce the physical stress of farmers at some level.

References

Bhattacharyya, N., & Chakrabarti, D. (2012). Ergonomic basket design to reduce cumulative trauma disorders in tea leaf plucking operation. *Work, 41*, 1234–1238.

Bibri, S. E. (2018). The IoT for smart sustainable cities of the future: An analytical framework for sensor-based big data applications for environmental sustainability. *Sustainable Cities and Society, 38*, 230–253.

Brandl, C., Mertens, A., & Schlick, C. M. (2017a). Effect of sampling interval on the reliability of ergonomic analysis using the Ovako working posture analysing system (OWAS). *International Journal of Industrial Ergonomics, 57*, 68–73. https://doi.org/10.1016/j.ergon.2016.11.013

Brandl, C., Mertens, A., & Schlick, C. M. (2017b). Ergonomic analysis of working postures using OWAS in semi-trailer assembly, applying an individual sampling strategy. *International Journal of Occupational Safety and Ergonomics (JOSE)*, 1–8. https://doi.org/10.1080/10803548.2016.1191224

Cakmak, B., Saracoglu, T., Alayunt, F. N., & Ozarslan, C. (2011). Vibration and noise characteristics of flap type olive harvesters. *Applied Ergonomics, 42*, 397–402.

CDC. (2013). *Agricultural safety*. Centers for Disease Control and Prevention. Retrieved from www.cdc.gov/niosh/topics/aginjury/

Chaturvedi, V., Kumar, A., & Singh, J. K. (2012). Power tiller: Vibration magnitudes and intervention development for vibration reduction. *Applied Ergonomics, 43*, 891–901. https://doi.org/10.1016/j.apergo.2011.12.012

Chavan, P. B., Patil, D. K., & Dhondge, D. S. (2015). Design and development of manually operated reaper. *IOSR Journal of Mechanical and Civil Engineering, 12*(3), 15–22.

Chieh-Tsung, C. (2012). A new electric brush cutter. *WSEAS Transactions on Systems and Control, 3*(7), 2224–2856.

Hamberg-van Reenen, H. H., Van Der Beek, A. J., Blatter, B. M., Van Der Grinten, M. P., Van Mechelen, W., Bongers, P. M. (2008). Does musculoskeletal discomfort at work predict future musculoskeletal pain?. *Ergonomics, 51*(5), 637–648.

Jatinder, K. J., & Rana, A. (2012). Ergonomic interventions in weeding operations for drudgery reduction of hill farm women of India. *Work, 41*, 4349–4355.

Karhu, O., Harkonen, R., Sorvali, P., & Vepsalainen, P. (1981). Observing working postures in industry: Examples of OWAS application. *Applied Ergonomics, 12*(1), 13–17. https://doi.org/10.1016/0003-6870(81)90088-0 (PMID:15676393).

Karhu, O., Kansi, P., & Kuorinka, I. (1977). Correcting working postures in industry: A practical method for analysis. *Applied Ergonomics, 8*(4), 199–201. https://doi.org/10.1016/0003-6870(77)90164-8 (PMID:15677243).

Kanjo, E., Younis, E. M., Sherkat, N. (2018). Towards unravelling the relationship between on-body, environmental and emotion data using sensor information fusion approach. *Information Fusion, 40*, 18–31.

Lovibond, P. F., Lovibond, S. H. (1995). The structure of negative emotional states: Comparison of the Depression Anxiety Stress Scales (DASS) with the Beck Depression and Anxiety Inventories. *Behaviour research and therapy, 33*(3), 335–343.

MATLAB. (2013). The MathWorks, Inc., Natick, Massachusetts, United States.

McAtamney, L., & Corlett, E. N. (1993). RULA: A survey method for the investigation of work related upper limb disorders. *Applied Ergonomics, 24*(2), 91–99.

Naeini, H. S., Karuppiah, K., Tamrin, S. B., & Dalal, K. (2014). Ergonomics in agriculture: An approach in prevention of work-related musculoskeletal disorders (WMSDs). *Journal of Agriculture and Environmental Sciences, 3*, 33–51.

Nunes, I. L. (2009). FAST ERGO_X—a tool for ergonomic auditing and work-related musculoskeletal disorders prevention. *WORK A Journal of Prevention, Assessment, and Rehabilitation, 34*(2), 133–148.

Patel, M. R., Peterson, E. D., Dai, D., Brennan, J. M., Redberg, R. F., Anderson, H. V., ... & Douglas, P. S. (2010). Low diagnostic yield of elective coronary angiography. *New England Journal of Medicine, 362*(10), 886–895.

Ren, J., & Xiao, D. (2009). Ergonomic simulation and evaluation of elliptical trainer with CATIA V5. *CADDM, 19*(1), 81–86.

Russo, M. A., Santarelli, D. M., & O'Rourke, D. (2017). The physiological effects of slow breathing in the healthy human. *Breathe, 13*(4), 298–309.

Sanjog, J., Karmakar, H., Agarwal, C., & Patil, D. (2012). Designing and ergonomic evaluation of a shoe-rack in CAD environment. *International Journal of Computer Applications, 49*(20), 38–41.

Trapp, M., Trapp, E. M., Egger, J. W., Domej, W., Schillaci, G., Avian, A., Baulmann, J. (2014). Impact of mental and physical stress on blood pressure and pulse pressure under normobaric versus hypoxic conditions. *PLoS One, 9*(5), e89005.

Vandermeer, J. M. (1992). *Thoughts on agriculture and the environment in a post-modern world. Symposium on enhancing the future of the land grant system.* National Academy of Sciences Board on Agriculture.

Vidyadhara, S., Chakravarthy, A., Pramod Kumar, A., Sriharsha, C., Rahul, R. (2020). Mental Health Status among the South Indian Pharmacy Students during Covid-19 Pandemic's Quarantine Period: A Cross-Sectional Study. *medRxiv preprint*. https://doi.org/10.1101/2020.05.08.20093708

Villarejo, D., Baron, S. L. (1999). The occupational health status of hired farm workers. *Occupational medicine (Philadelphia, Pa.), 14*(3), 613–635.

Wright, A. L., Dou, F., & Hons, F. M. (2007). Soil organic C and N distribution for wheat cropping systems after 20 years of conservation tillage in central Texas. *Systems and Environment, 121*, 376–382.

Zolfani, S. H., Bahrami, M. (2014). Investment prioritizing in high tech industries based on swara-copras approach. *Technological and Economic Development of Economy, 20*(3), 534–533. https://doi.org/10.3846/20294913.2014.881435

Chapter 4
Risk and Mental Health Assessment for Construction and Mining Workers

Abstract In particular, construction and mining workers suffer from diseases like respiratory and skin diseases due to an unhealthy atmosphere. Risk factors related to work are also very high due to the type of work. The construction and mining sectors are both labour-intensive sectors. Large numbers of workers doing manual labour in a dusty and polluted climate. Many of the works performed are repetitive and heavy working nature. So, most workers face back pain, shoulder pain, body pain and musculoskeletal disorders (MSDs). The main cause of hazards is unhealthy workplaces in the mining and construction sector. But the mining and construction industries were the symbol of the growth of a country. But the risks associated with the mining sector and the construction sector are also very high. The risk of hazards, accidents are maximum in both these sectors. So an effort is taken to study and prioritize risk factors in the mining sector and construction sector.

Keywords Mental stress · Risk · Ranking · Prediction · Construction worker · Mining worker

4.1 Introduction

Miners have to work inside mines, and it is considered the most dangerous job compared to others. Usually, mines are away from residence and demand a strenuous job shift wise. The mining environment is also not healthy. Exposure to dust and chemical substances, high temperatures, humidity, noise, vibration, etc. creates an unsuitable environment. More physical work, shift jobs, high job demand, isolation from family, injuries, accidents, and musculoskeletal pain due to heavy and repetitive jobs make miners mentally sick and increase psychological pressure. Usually, mining workers suffer from pulmonary disorders due to exposure to dust and small particles of asbestos, minerals, hazardous gases, etc. It not only causes asthma and skin cancer, but also eye irritation and burning sensations. The high noise and vibration inside mines and the unhealthy atmosphere are the main causes of cardiovascular diseases among miners. Miners suffer great pain due to MSDs (musculoskeletal disorders).

S. Satapathy et al., *Occupational Health Safety Factors and Their Impact on the Mental Health of Workers*, New Perspectives in Behavioral & Health Sciences,
https://doi.org/10.1007/978-981-99-7619-5_4

Injuries and accidents due to the failure of structures while working with machines are very common. Nakua et al. (2019) have discovered that 25.8% of miners were injured inside a mine. Basu et al. (2015) found that 50% of miners in a mine were suffering from stress, body pain, cardiovascular disorders, hypertension, etc. Bauerle et al. (2018) have investigated and wrote that due to the FIFO (fly in, fly out) system to improve mining work, miners were under stress and not getting family time, leisure time, or even sufficient sleep. Wang et al. (2010), Paech et al. (2010), Ferguson et al. (2011), Carlisle and Parker (2014), Deng et al. (2017), Yu et al. (2017), James et al. (2018), Pelders and Nelson (2019) have investigated and found a relationship between physical disorder, work organization pressure, and mental disorder (stress). Caldwell et al. (2019) have written that sleepiness is the main cause of physical tiredness. Garbarino et al. (2016) have explained that injuries and accidents are at their highest when miners feel tired due to a lack of sleep. Etuknwa et al. (2019) have found that the outcome of MSD is mental sickness, and Zhao et al. (2019) and Brown et al. (2020) have explained that lengthy shift work has adverse effects on sleep, consciousness about safety, and mental wellness.

4.2 Research Methodology for Mining Workers

To study and access the risk and mental wellness of mining workers, a standard question (Table 4.1) is designed from extensive literature review and circulated among different mining workers in Mexico, Nigeria, Ethiopia, Malaysia, Ghana, South Africa, and India by mail and personal interview. The datasets were collected by Likert scale 1–5 (i.e. 1 = totally disagree, 2 = somewhat disagree, 3 = no opinion, 4 = somewhat agree, 5 = totally agree). Among the 240 sets of questions, 212 responses were received from coal, copper, bauxite, and iron mines, which was 88% and acceptable.

From Figs. 4.1 and 4.2, it is found that maximum data is collected from India and coalmines. All the workers worked in the same mines for 5–10 years or more and their aged between 22 and 42 years. Then statistical analysis is conducted to assess the mental health of mining workers.

4.3 Results and Discussion by WASPAS Method for Mining Sector

The factor analysis is conducted with Minitab 17 software for the collected 212 datasets under four dimensions (psychological problems due to personal issues, psychological problems due to health issues, physical problems, and workplace issues and quality of life and well-being) (Fig. 4.2). Seventeen variables were selected under the above 4 dimensions/constructs having a Cronbach's alpha value of 0.5, and more

Table 4.1 Question

Question	1	2	3	4	5
Job pressure of miner					
Sleep disorderliness					
Individual characteristics and behaviour					
Chronic or hereditary mental disease					
Neuropsychological imbalance					
Drugs/wine consumption					
Interpersonal abstraction					
Psychosocial threats and risk					
Hereditary or individual health issue					
Job satisfaction					
Good quality of life					
Workplace and family well-being					
Musculoskeletal disorder or body pain due to physical work					
More shift job so less rest					
Injuries and accidents					
Workplace safety					
Organization culture and variables					
Financial issue					
Job in security and difficult in resisting or coping with workplace					
Quarrel at workplace					

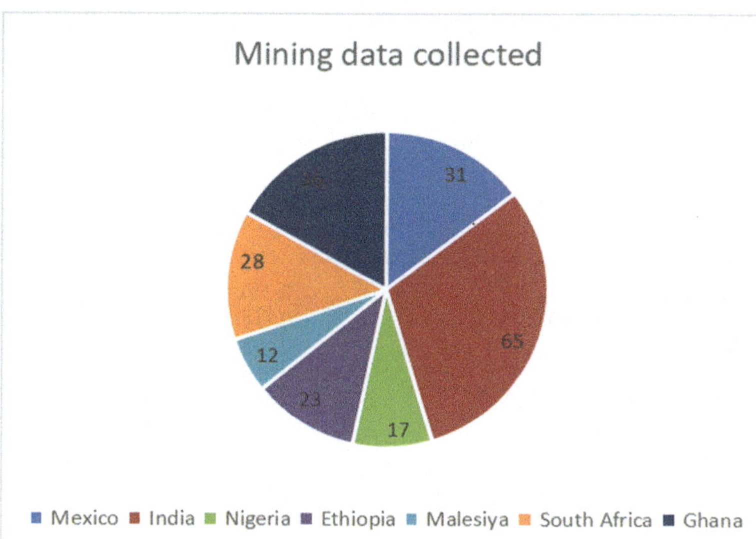

Fig. 4.1 Amount of data collected from different mines from different countries

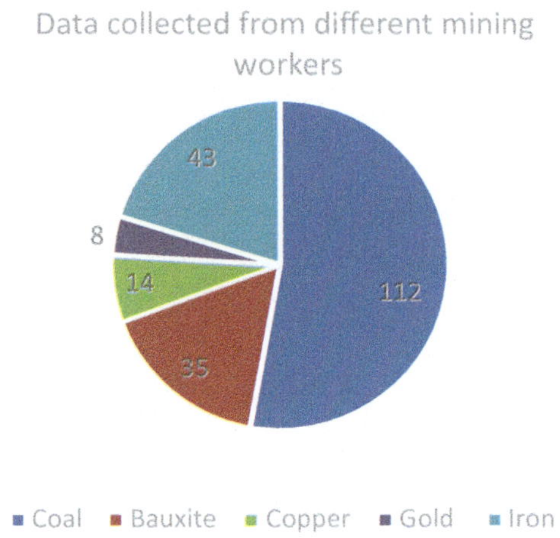

Fig. 4.2 Mines covered for collecting data

and the rest 3 variables were discarded. Table 4.3 shows names of constructs and items (Table 4.2).

Table 4.2 Factor analysis

Factors	Items	Factor 1	Factor 2	Factor 3	Factor 4	Cronbach's alpha
Psychological problems due to personal issues (Pizarro & Fuenzalida, 2021)	1, 2, 3, 4, 5	0.601, 0.504, 0.867, 0.752, 0.501				0.523 0.612 0.527 0.538 0.615
Psychological problems due to health issues (Pizarro & Fuenzalida, 2021)	6, 7, 8, 9		0.503, 0.511, 0.732, 0.809			0.540 0.563 0.603 0.608
Physical problems and workplace issue (Pizarro & Fuenzalida, 2021)	13, 14, 15, 16, 17			0.736, 0.718, 0.693, 0.624, 0.567		0.568 0.595 0.831 0.845
Quality of life and well-being (Pizarro & Fuenzalida, 2021)	10, 11, 12				0.555 0.610 0.529	0.764 0.700 0.663
Variance		3.3428	2.4146	1.9733	1.0702	
% Var		0.273	0.254	0.225	0.178	

Then the WASPAS method is implemented to prioritize the most important risk and mental pressure for mining workers. Zavadskas et al. (2012) have created the WASPAS method. This method is an accurate MCDM approach, which can improve the ranking of alternatives. It is the combination of the Weighted Product Model (WPM) and the Weighted Sum Model (WSM). The WASPAS method has application in a variety of fields. A hybrid method presented is used by combining WASPAS and entropy methods to develop airport based on the calculation. Have formulated a combine model supported by fuzzy WASPAS and fuzzy AHP to determine retail centre.

Step 1 **First, a j**udgmental matrix is established

The judgment matrix X_{ij} shows the relation of criteria to alternatives.

Step 2 Normalization of decision matrix

Beneficial and non-beneficial criteria are decided by the decision-maker.

$$\overline{X}_{ij} = \frac{X_{ij}}{\mathrm{Max}i\, X_{ij}} \text{ for beneficial criteria} \tag{4.1}$$

$$\overline{X}_{ij} = \frac{\mathrm{Min}i\, X_{ij}}{X_{ij}} \text{ for non-beneficial criteria,} \tag{4.2}$$

Table 4.3 Name of items

Item no	Name of variables
1	Job pressure of miner
2	Sleep disorderliness
3	Individual characteristics and behaviour
4	Chronic or hereditary mental disease
5	Neuro psychological imbalance
6	Drugs/wine consumption
7	Interpersonal abstraction
8	Psychosocial threats and risk
9	Hereditary or individual health issue
10	Job satisfaction
11	Good quality of life
12	Workplace and family well-being
13	Musculoskeletal disorder or body pain due to physical work
14	More shift job so less rest
15	Injuries and accidents
16	Workplace safety
17	Organization culture and variables

$\overline{X}_{ij}$ normalized value is calculated in the second step.

Step 3 **The** WSM method is used to find relative performance.

The WSM method was developed by MacCrimon (1968) Triantaphyllou and Mann (1989). W_j is the weight (relative weight) of the jth criterion.

Step 4 **Wpm model is used to find** relative performances of alternatives

$$Q_i(1) = \prod_{j=1}^{n} (\overline{X}_{ij}) W_{ij} \tag{4.3}$$

Step 5 **Finally**, the combination of WPM and WSM is used to find performance of alternatives from 0 to 1.

$$Q_i = 0.5P_i^{(1)} + 0.5P_i^{(2)} \tag{4.4}$$

$$Q_i = \alpha P_i^{(1)} + (1 - \alpha)P_i^{(2)} \tag{4.5}$$

Step 6: Ranking of alternatives

Lastly, ranking is done to find the most important challenges. Tables 4.4, 4.5 and 4.6 show steps of WASPAS ranking.

Workplace safety is the main risk for psychological and physical disorder. Hence, the workplace must be redesigned and modified with advanced technologies, and workers must be provided with personal protective equipment to keep them safe. Regular counselling and health checkup can reduce the risk of mental risk for mining workers.

4.4 Construction Sector Risk

Construction industries are in high demand in both developed and developing countries. As infrastructure growth (i.e. growth of business centres, industries, hotels, malls), the growth of residential (i.e. apartments, independent houses) and non-residential plots such as roads and dams are essential worldwide for both developed and developing countries. Green construction industries are in high demand and also necessary for environmental and human safety. Sustainable construction industries play a vital role in the occupational safety of all kinds of construction workers (i.e. masons, welders, carpenters, skilled and unskilled labourers). Construction work is heavy, repetitive in nature. It is also very dangerous for human health. Many of the workers suffered from muscular disorders, skin problems due to reactions to chemicals, burning eye problems in welding, cuts, and wounds due to the use of tools in the carpentry section. Although many risks and hazards are found in

Table 4.4 Decision matrix

Job pressure of miner	4.555	3.111	3.888	2.7777	3.666	4.555
Sleep disorderliness	3.888	4.111	3.666	3.444	3.555	4.111
Individual characteristics and behaviour	4.555	3.555	3.4444	3.6666	3.333	4.5555
Chronic or hereditary mental disease	4.111	3.555	3.5555	3.5555	3.888	4.1111
Neuro psychological imbalance	4.555	2.6666	3.7777	2.8888	4	4.5555
Drugs/wine consumption	4.666	3.1111	4	3.3333	4.555	4.6666
Interpersonal abstraction	3.333	3.6666	3.44444	3.1111	3.888	3.888
Psychosocial threats and risk	3.555	4	4.1111	3.4444	4.555	4.555
Hereditary or individual health issue	4.111	4.5555	3.1111	3.8888	4.111	4.5555
Job satisfaction	3.888	3.8888	4.1111	2.6666	4.555	4.5555
Good quality of life	3.666	4.5555	3.5555	2.8888	4.666	4.6666
Workplace and family well-being	3.444	4.1111	3.5555	2.6666	3.333	4.1111
Musculoskeletal disorder or body pain due to physical work	3.555	4.555	2.6666	3.4444	3.555	4.5555
More shift job so less rest	3.777	4.666	3.1111	4	4.111	4.6666
Injuries and accidents	4	3.333	3.6666	3.1111	3.888	4
Workplace safety	3.444	3.555	3.444	3	3.666	3.6666
Organization culture and variables	4.111	4.111	3.7777	3.3333	3.444	4.1111

construction work, still many of the countries and construction industries are still the basis of their growth and prosperity. Many of the prosperous countries follow sustainability in the construction sector, and still some countries are away from it. To identify the risk and hazards in the construction industry, a survey is conducted and a framework is designed to reduce the most important risk factors with sustainability tools. In developing countries, such as India, 44 million construction workers are found, many of whom are unskilled and handle multidisciplinary construction work (i.e. painting, polishing roads, loading–unloading of cement, sand, mixtures, bricks, braking stones, lifting rods, etc.). Skilled workers handle carpentry, welding, mason jobs, etc., but unskilled and semiskilled workers used to do assigned helping jobs without proper training. Many of the construction workers are not regular construction workers, most of the time in the off-season, when no agriculture work, for their bread and butter are engaged themself in construction work either on a daily wage basis or on contractual basis as migrant labour. Construction work usually varies in nature from citing to cite or project to project starting from road, dam, industry and housing projects, etc. In developing countries, such as India, 44 million construction workers are found, many of whom are unskilled and handle multidisciplinary construction works (i.e. painting, polishing roads, loading–unloading of cement, sands, mixtures, bricks, braking stones, lifting rods). Skilled workers handle carpentry, welding, mason jobs, etc., but unskilled and semiskilled workers used to do assigned helping jobs without proper training. Many of the construction workers are not regular construction workers, most of the time in the off-season, when no

Table 4.5 Normalized value

	A (coal)	B (Bauxite)	C (Coper)	D (Gold)	E (Iron)
Job pressure of miner	1	0.6829	0.8536	0.609	0.8048
Sleep disorderliness	0.9459	1	0.891891892	0.837837838	0.864864865
Individual characteristics and behaviour	1	0.780487805	0.756097561	0.804878049	0.731707317
Chronic or hereditary mental disease	1	0.864864865	0.864864865	0.864864865	0.945945946
Neuropsychological imbalance	1	0.585365854	0.829268293	0.634146341	0.87804878
Drugs/wine consumption	1	0.666666667	0.857142857	0.714285714	0.976190476
Interpersonal abstraction	0.857142857	0.942857143	0.885714285	0.8	1
Psychosocial threats and risk	0.87804878	0.902439024	0.756097561	1	1
Hereditary or individual health issue	1	0.682926829	0.853658537	0.902439024	1
Job satisfaction	0.853658537	0.902439024	0.585365854	1	1
Good quality of life	0.785714286	0.976190476	0.761904762	0.619047619	1
Workplace and family well-being	0.837837838	1	0.864864865	0.648648649	0.810810811
Musculoskeletal disorder or body pain due to physical work	0.780487805	1	0.585365854	0.756097561	0.780487805
More shift job so less rest	0.809523809	1	0.666666667	0.857142857	0.880952381
Injuries and accidents	1	0.833333333	0.916666667	0.777777778	0.972222222
Workplace safety	0.939393939	0.96969697	0.939393939	0.818181818	1
Organization culture and variables	0.995158687	1	0.914470145	0.806885422	0.833781603

agriculture work, for their bread and butter are engaged themselves in construction work either on a daily wage basis or on contractual basis as migrant labour. Construction work usually varies in nature from citing to cite or project to project starting from road, dam, industry, housing projects, etc. As per ILO, the mortality cases, accidents, and hazard percentages are very high in a construction jobs. For the sake of high wages, the untrained and uneducated young masses without personal

Table 4.6 Ranking of risk factors in mining

Q1	Q2	Q		Rank
0.790243902	0.778590176	0.784417039	Job pressure of miner	
0.908108108	0.906269475	0.907188791	Sleep disorderliness	5
0.814634146	0.809472852	0.812053499	Individual characteristics and behaviour	
0.908108108	0.906446584	0.907277346	Chronic or hereditary mental disease	4
0.785365854	0.769779101	0.777572477	Neuropsychological imbalance	
0.842857143	0.831904927	0.837381035	Drugs/wine consumption	
0.897142857	0.89449218	0.895817519	Interpersonal abstraction	
0.907317073	0.902615672	0.904966372	Psychosocial threats and risk	3
0.887804878	0.879458288	0.883631583	Hereditary or individual health issue	
0.868292683	0.852758168	0.860525425	Job satisfaction	
0.828571429	0.815989917	0.822280673	Good quality of life	
0.832432432	0.824531885	0.828482159	Workplace and family well-being	
0.780487805	0.769391693	0.774939749	Musculoskeletal disorder or body pain due to physical work	
0.842857143	0.835658437	0.83925779	More shift job so less rest	
0.9	0.896045893	0.898022946	Injuries and accidents	
0.933333333	0.931185649	0.932259491	Workplace safety	1
0.910059172	0.906536322	0.908297747	Organization culture and variables	2

protection kits are forced to engage themselves in short-term construction site risky jobs by private contractors. As the jobs are not regularized, the type of work also changes from time to time and place to place. The United States Bureau of Labour Statistics (2019) has found that at the US construction site in between 2003 and 2016 approximately, 12,500 workers died in the workplace due to accidents. Most of the workers in the construction sites are not alert of regulations, their rights, insurance, and claims against injustice. High noise and vibration in the workplace deteriorate the nervous system and reduces the mental and physical power of the chemicals, dust particles of asbestos, granite powders, tile, and marble chips to create eye contagion and pulmonary diseases: however, they work uncomplainingly in unhealthy environmental conditions.

Therefore, a survey is conducted, and the workplace risks of Indian workers involved in different construction sites are studied and prioritized. Then, QEC ergonomic analysis is performed for the most difficult construction jobs in India. Albert et al. (2014) found that 50% of workers and more are unaware of risk and hazards in construction workplaces. Recommended multiple hazard analysis techniques due to their own strength and weakness. Safety training is always provided in industries; however, the effectiveness of lecture-based training is a major question by a few researchers, such as Bhandari et al. (2019), Jeelani et al. (2017a, 2017b), and Hung et al. (2013).

Agumba and Haupt (2008) and Rwamamara et al. (2007) found that compared to all other industrial workers, construction workers face two times more work-related injuries and illnesses. Schneider (2001) and Golabchi et al. (2015) found that, due to the highest worker injury, fatality rates, and work-related musculoskeletal disorders (WMSDs) faced by the construction sector, the satisfaction and working capacity of construction workers decreases. Ajayi and HwDlD (2012) explored that musculoskeletal disorders (MSD) problems are the most current form of occupational health problem. Kebrit and Rani (2013) found that 25% of workers face backache and 23% suffer from muscular pain in European Union (EU) countries in construction projects, so workers remain absent most of the time due to MSDs in the US. Loewenson (1999) explored that, out of five workers, one worker in the Swedish construction industry has suffered from WMSDs and 69% reported construction work-related injuries in 2005.

4.5 Methodology II for Construction Sector

To study hazard factors at construction sites, a study was performed with the research group, in Odisha (India). For this study, a committee was formed with supervisors of particular research, two trained research scholars (one male and one female) with approval with KIIT institution research committee and construction site project officers. This study was conducted for six months 2021 February to 2021 August for workers of age above 20, no minors were considered for this survey. The construction site workers have given their consent to publish their images in this research. The research committee was instructed to only observe and record working procedures and postures without disturbing their routine work and following all rules and regulations. Four construction sites were selected, where some construction works were going on. A standard questionnaire was designed with the help of experts in academic and literature reviews and consisted of 20 risk factors related to the construction sites (Appendix 1). A survey was conducted, by personal contact with 204 workers in their local language, who were engaged in construction projects with their consent. The workers, who were engaged for 10–15 years in construction sites and between age 20 and 40 years, are interviewed. Then, the data were gathered to discover the no of injuries/hazards found in the workplace. The risk factors at construction sites are prioritized by additive ratio assessment (ARAS) multicriteria decision-making method.

Appendix-1

Question	1	2	3	4	5
Job pressure					
Sleep disorderliness					
Individual characteristics and behaviour					
Chronic or hereditary mental disease					
Neuro psychological imbalance					
Drugs/wine consumption					
Interpersonal abstraction					
Pshycosocial threats and risk					
Hereditary or individual health issue					
Job satisfaction					
Good quality of life					
Workplace and family well being					
Musculoskeletal disorder or body pain due to physical work					
More shift job so less rest					
Injuries and accidents					
Work place safety					
Organization culture and variables					
Financial issue					
Job in security and difficult in resisting or coping with work place					
Quarrel at workplace					

The ARAS method is utilized in science, business, and government. It helps to work on the nature of choices by settling on the dynamic interaction more effectively. It is the fastest developing field of activity research. It has the capacity to resolve the different dynamic issues by time-bound application.

4.6 Results and Discussion for Construction Site

To identify the most important risk factor in the construction site, 51 workers were chosen from each site, a total of 204 workers were selected and factor analysis was conducted by Minitab 17, with respect to six occupational risks or hazard constructs. The variable with more than 0.5 ronbach's alpha values is elected as the most dangerous risk parameter for construction project workers. Among the 20 items, 15 variables were designated under six risk dimensions and 5 variables below. Five values were discarded as not relevant. The constructs chosen are ergonomic risk, biological risk, physical risk, chemical risk, safety risk, and psychosocial risks. The factor analysis result is cited in Appendix 2. Then the ARAS multicriteria decision-making method was followed with the entropy method to weight calculation to rank the risk factors.

Appendix-2

Factor	Item	F1	F2	F3	F4	F5	F6
Ergonomic risks	• Workplace and family well being	0.567					
	• Musculoskeletal disorder or body pain due to physical work	0.534					
	• Interpersonal abstraction	0.512					
Chemical hazards	• Neuro psychological imbalance		0.571				
Biological hazards	• Pshycosocial threats and risk			0.511			
Physical hazards	• Injuries and accidents				0.508		
	• Job pressure				0.507		
	• Quarrel at workplace				0.601		
Safety hazards	• More shift job so less rest					0.501	
	• Work place safety					0.612	
	• Job in security and difficult in resisting or coping with work place					0.632	
Psycho social risks	• Pshycosocial threats and risk						0.520
	• Sleep disorderliness						0.519
	• Chronic or hereditary mental disease						0.549
	• Individual characteristics and behaviour						0.572

Step 1: Find the optimum value X_{0j} of risk factor
Step 2: Find the normalized value R_{ij}
where R_{ij} represent as normalized value
Step 3: Calculate the weighted R_{ij} value
Step 4: Calculate the total performance index
Step 5: Find the degree of utility, $S_o = 1$
Step 6: Prioritize the risk factors

Table 4.7 shows the percentage of risk factors data collected for construction projects, where construction sector A represents housing projects, construction Project B shows road construction project, construction Project C is for bridge construction project and construction Project D means industry construction projects.

Construction sector A and construction Project B are denoted as not regulated as these projects are done by maximum by privatized or contractual basis but C and D are always done with abiding rules and regulation of Govt. concerns or with industrial concerns. Table 4.8 shows normalized value obtained with considering optimum value for construction sites A and B, and Table 4.8 shows the normalized value of construction sites C and D, respectively. Tables 4.9 and 4.10 represents the normalized value and weighted normalized value of four construction sectors for risk factors considering weights. Lastly, Table 4.11 is the ranking table nominated ergonomics risk is the most dangerous risk for construction site workers.

w1 (0.249), w2 (0.244), w3 (0.251), and w4 (0.254) are calculated by the entropy method.

From Table 4.12, it is found that ergonomics risk is the most prioritized risk ranked and biological risk and physical risk become the 2nd and 3rd criteria of

Table 4.7 Percentage of construction workers risk

	Construction site A (NB = not regulated)	Construction site B (NB = not regulated)	Construction site C	Construction site D
Ergonomic risks	54.5	55	54	67.4
Chemical hazards	60.66	61.3	67.1	61
Biological hazards	58	58.3	61.3	61.6
Physical hazards	56	58	58	59
Safety hazards	65.3	65.3	62	61
Psychosocial risks	63	61.5	62	64

Table 4.8 Normalized value of construction workers

	Construction site (NB = not regulated)	Construction site B (NB = not regulated)	Construction site C	Construction site D
OV	65.3	65.3	54	59
Ergonomic risks	54.5	55	54	67.4
Chemical hazards	60.66	61.3	67.1	61
Biological hazards	58	58.3	61.3	61.6
Physical hazards	56	58	58	59
Safety hazards	65.3	65.3	62	61
Psychosocial risks	63	61.5	62	64

Table 4.9 Normalized value of non-beneficial criteria

	Construction site C	Construction site D
OV	0.018518519	0.016949153
Ergonomic risks	0.016129032	0.016393443
Chemical hazards	0.01490313	0.016393443
Biological hazards	0.016313214	0.016233766
Physical hazards	0.017241379	0.016949153
Safety hazards	0.018518519	0.014836795
Psychosocial risks	0.016129032	0.015625

Table 4.10 Normalized value for construction workers

	Construction site (NB = not regulated)	Construction site B (NB = not regulated)	Construction site C	Construction site D
OV	0.15446116	0.153755592	0.157266024	0.1494888
Ergonomic risks	0.182677782	0.181691708	0.162534843	0.170000734
Chemical hazards	0.207625958	0.208432506	0.179328327	0.204820342
Biological hazards	0.250372903	0.250264263	0.152941675	0.160474428
Physical hazards	0.322140599	0.331740507	0.126927416	0.131124407
Safety hazards	0.461689259	0.469909235	0.108744391	0.090929304
Psychosocial risks	0.987536075	0.987251706	0.075327652	0.074619327

Table 4.11 Weighted normalized value

	Construction site (NB = not regulated)	Construction site B (NB = not regulated)	Construction site C	Construction site D
Weight	0.249	0.244	0.251	0.254
OV		0.037516364	0.039473772	0.037970155
Ergonomic risks	0.045486768	0.044332777	0.040796245	0.043180186
Chemical hazards	0.051698864	0.050857531	0.04501141	0.204820342
Biological hazards	0.062342853	0.06106448	0.03838836	0.040760505
Physical hazards	0.080213009	0.080944684	0.031858781	0.033305599
Safety hazards	0.114960625	0.114657853	0.027294842	0.023096043
Psychosocial risks	0.245896483	0.240889416	0.018907241	0.018953309

risk. As ergonomics risk is the most important risk, analysis is performed by QEC assessment tool on the basis of images taken of the most difficult and repetitive work in different types of construction sites.

Figure 4.1 shows the image of stone collectors in an industrial site. Figure 4.2 is the question obtained by visualizing the body's posture during this particular job, and Fig. 4.3 calculates the score obtained by QEC questions in Fig. 4.2. Lastly, a graph is prepared in Fig. 4.4 by considering the body parts position and total score.

Figure 4.3 shows the image of stone collectors in an industrial site. Figure 4.4 is the question obtained by visualizing the body's posture during this particular job, and Fig. 4.5 calculates the score obtained by QEC questions of Fig. 4.4. Lastly, a graph is prepared in Fig. 4.6 by considering the body parts position and total score.

Figure 4.7 loading and unloading images, Fig. 4.8 converts to questionnaire form in QEC. Figures 4.9 and 4.10 shows the scores obtained by QEC and a graph of body parts score

Figure 4.11 shows the image of a worker during bridge construction in tilted and bend position taking measurements. Figure 4.12 converts this posture in terms of QEC questionnaire, Fig. 4.13 to scores and Fig. 4.14 represents in terms of graph.

Table 4.12 Ranking of risk factors

	Si	So	K	Rank
	0.153421121	0.153421121	1	
Ergonomic risks	0.173795976		0.882765665	1
Chemical hazards	0.352388147		0.435375372	5
Biological hazards	0.202556198		0.757424961	2
Physical hazards	0.226322074		0.677888454	3
Safety hazards	0.280009364		0.54791425	4
Psychosocial risks	0.524646449		0.292427636	6

Fig. 4.3 Stone collecting in construction site (industry)

Worker's name ______ Date ______

Observer's Assessment

Back

A When performing the task, is the back *(select worse case situation)*
- A1 Almost neutral?
- A2 Moderately flexed or twisted or side bent?
- A3 ✓ Excessively flexed or twisted or side bent?

B Select ONLY ONE of the two following task options:

EITHER

For seated or standing stationary tasks. Does the back remain in a static position most of the time?
- B1 No
- B2 ✓ Yes

OR

For lifting, pushing/pulling and carrying tasks (i.e. moving a load). Is the movement of the back
- B3 Infrequent (around 3 times per minute or less)?
- B4 Frequent (around 8 times per minute)?
- B5 ✓ Very frequent (around 12 times per minute or more)?

Shoulder/Arm

C When the task is performed, are the hands *(select worse case situation)*
- C1 ✓ At or below waist height?
- C2 At about chest height?
- C3 At or above shoulder height?

D Is the shoulder/arm movement
- D1 Infrequent (some intermittent movement)?
- D2 ✓ Frequent (regular movement with some pauses)?
- D3 Very frequent (almost continuous movement)?

Wrist/Hand

E Is the task performed with *(select worse case situation)*
- E1 An almost straight wrist?
- E2 ✓ A deviated or bent wrist?

F Are similar motion patterns repeated
- F1 ✓ 10 times per minute or less?
- F2 11 to 20 times per minute?
- F3 More than 20 times per minute?

Neck

G When performing the task, is the head/neck bent or twisted?
- G1 No
- G2 Yes, occasionally
- G3 ✓ Yes, continuously

Worker's Assessment

Workers

H Is the maximum weight handled MANUALLY BY YOU in this task?
- H1 ✓ Light (5 kg or less)
- H2 Moderate (6 to 10 kg)
- H3 Heavy (11 to 20kg)
- H4 Very heavy (more than 20 kg)

J On average, how much time do you spend per day on this task?
- J1 Less than 2 hours
- J2 2 to 4 hours
- J3 ✓ More than 4 hours

K When performing this task, is the maximum force level exerted by one hand?
- K1 ✓ Low (e.g. less than 1 kg)
- K2 Medium (e.g. 1 to 4 kg)
- K3 High (e.g. more than 4 kg)

L Is the visual demand of this task
- L1 Low (almost no need to view fine details)?
- *L2 ✓ High (need to view some fine details)?

** If High, please give details in the box below*

M At work do you drive a vehicle for
- M1 ✓ Less than one hour per day or Never?
- M2 Between 1 and 4 hours per day?
- M3 More than 4 hours per day?

N At work do you use vibrating tools for
- N1 ✓ Less than one hour per day or Never?
- N2 Between 1 and 4 hours per day?
- N3 More than 4 hours per day?

P Do you have difficulty keeping up with this work?
- P1 Never
- P2 ✓ Sometimes
- *P3 Often

** If Often, please give details in the box below*

Q In general, how do you find this job
- Q1 Not at all stressful?
- Q2 Mildly stressful?
- *Q3 ✓ Moderately stressful?
- *Q4 Very stressful?

** If Moderately or Very, please give details in the box below*

** Additional details for L, P and Q if appropriate*

*L

*P ✓

*Q

Fig. 4.4 QEC analysis for stone collection

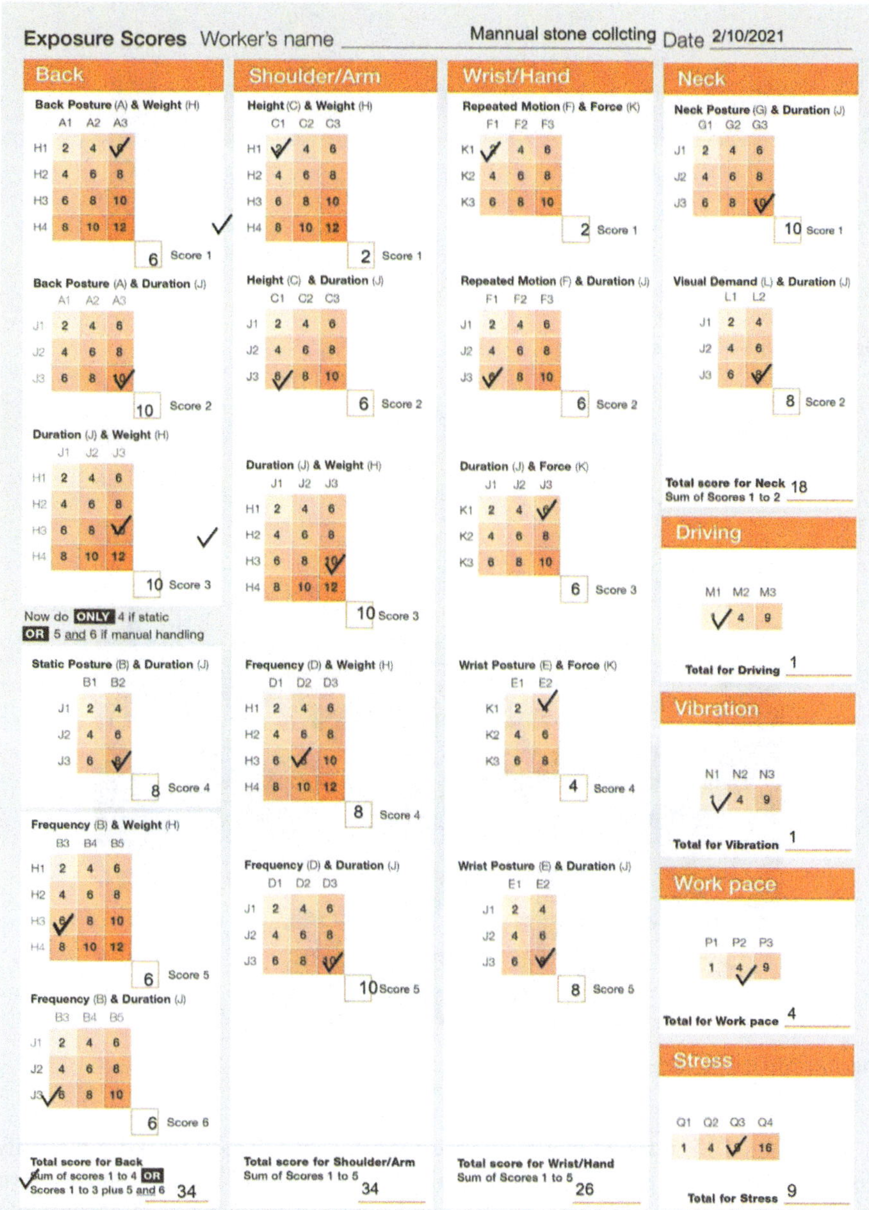

Fig. 4.5 Stone collection QEC score

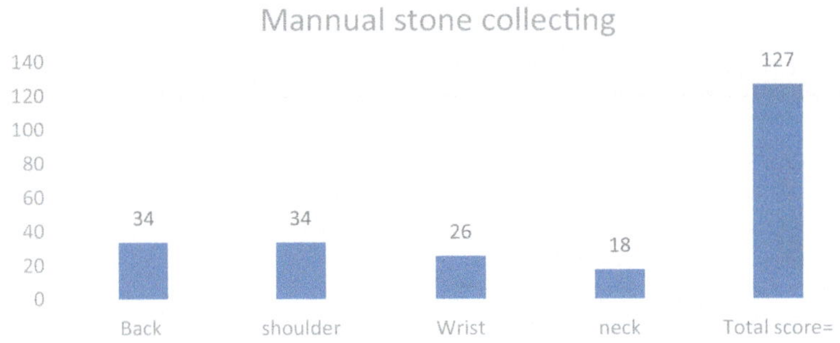

Fig. 4.6 Graph of QEC score

Fig. 4.7 Mixture loading

From Fig. 4.15, it found that the workers are engaged in road work for 8 h daily. Figure 4.16 converts the observation obtained from Fig. 4.17 to questionnaire form in Fig. 4.16. Figure 4.18 explains the score obtained from the road construction questionnaire of Fig. 4.16 and actual image Fig. 4.15. Figure 4.18 shows the effect of this bend posture, leg position in terms of a graph showing the scores.

QEC questionnaire that explains the head, shoulder, neck, hand, etc. positions respectively during work. Finally, graphs are plotted to show the risk posture while

Worker's name worker 2 engaged in mixture loading Date 2/10/2021

Observer's Assessment

Back

A When performing the task, is the back
(select worse case situation)
A1 ✓ Almost neutral?
A2 Moderately flexed or twisted or side bent?
A3 Excessively flexed or twisted or side bent?

B Select ONLY ONE of the two following task options:
EITHER
For seated or standing stationary tasks. Does the back remain in a static position most of the time?
B1 No
B2 ✓ Yes
OR
For lifting, pushing/pulling and carrying tasks (i.e. moving a load). Is the movement of the back
B3 Infrequent (around 3 times per minute or less)?
B4 ✓ Frequent (around 8 times per minute)?
B5 Very frequent (around 12 times per minute or more)?

Shoulder/Arm

C When the task is performed, are the hands
(select worse case situation)
C1 At or below waist height?
C2 At about chest height?
C3 ✓ At or above shoulder height?

D Is the shoulder/arm movement
D1 Infrequent (some intermittent movement)?
D2 ✓ Frequent (regular movement with some pauses)?
D3 Very frequent (almost continuous movement)?

Wrist/Hand

E Is the task performed with
(select worse case situation)
E1 An almost straight wrist?
E2 ✓ A deviated or bent wrist?

F Are similar motion patterns repeated
F1 10 times per minute or less?
F2 11 to 20 times per minute?
F3 ✓ More than 20 times per minute?

Neck

G When performing the task, is the head/neck bent or twisted?
G1 No
G2 ✓ Yes, occasionally
G3 Yes, continuously

Worker's Assessment

Workers

H Is the maximum weight handled MANUALLY BY YOU in this task?
H1 Light (5 kg or less)
H2 ✓ Moderate (6 to 10 kg)
H3 Heavy (11 to 20kg)
H4 Very heavy (more than 20 kg)

J On average, how much time do you spend per day on this task?
J1 Less than 2 hours
J2 2 to 4 hours
J3 ✓ More than 4 hours

K When performing this task, is the maximum force level exerted by one hand?
K1 Low (e.g. less than 1 kg)
K2 Medium (e.g. 1 to 4 kg)
K3 ✓ High (e.g. more than 4 kg)

L Is the visual demand of this task
L1 Low (almost no need to view fine details)?
*L2 ✓ High (need to view some fine details)?
* *If High, please give details in the box below*

M At work do you drive a vehicle for
M1 ✓ Less than one hour per day or Never?
M2 Between 1 and 4 hours per day?
M3 More than 4 hours per day?

N At work do you use vibrating tools for
N1 ✓ Less than one hour per day or Never?
N2 Between 1 and 4 hours per day?
N3 More than 4 hours per day?

P Do you have difficulty keeping up with this work?
P1 Never
P2 ✓ Sometimes
*P3 Often
* *If Often, please give details in the box below*

Q In general, how do you find this job
Q1 Not at all stressful?
Q2 Mildly stressful?
*Q3 ✓ Moderately stressful?
*Q4 Very stressful?
* *If Moderately or Very, please give details in the box below*

* *Additional details for L, P and Q if appropriate*
*L
*P
*Q ✓

Fig. 4.8 QEC questionnaire of loading mixture

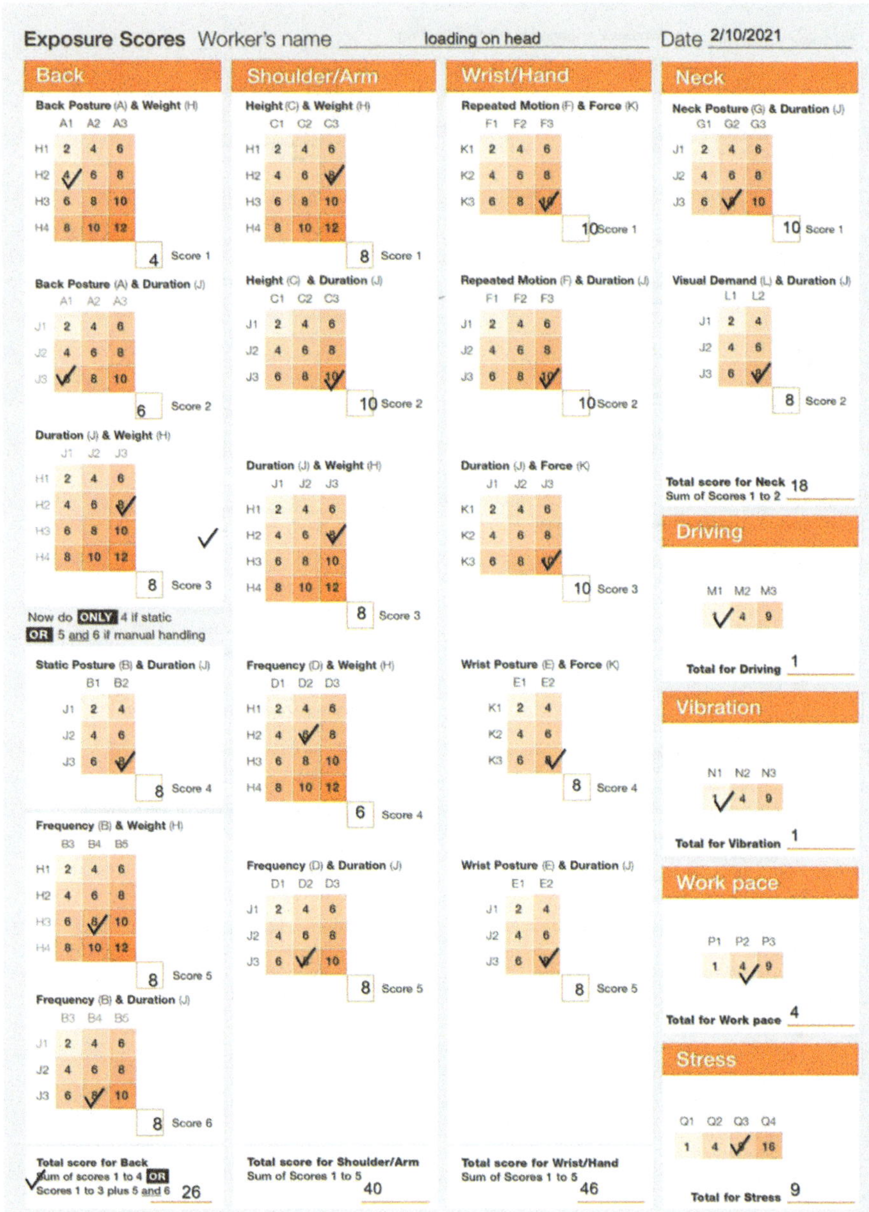

Fig. 4.9 QEC score of loading mixture

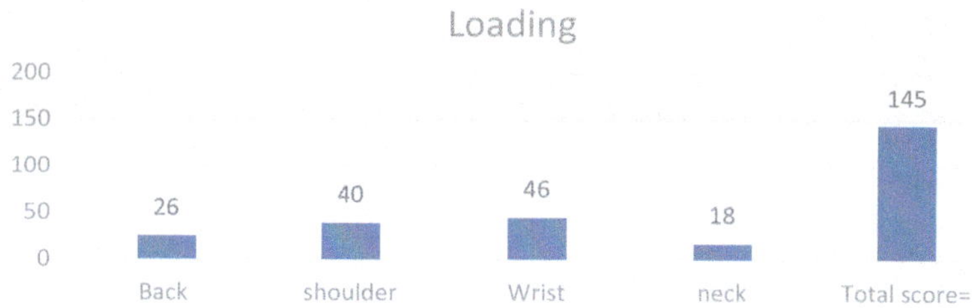

Fig. 4.10 Graph of QEC score in loading

Fig. 4.11 Dam construction

working. And it shows that road construction workers are at high risk due to repetitive work in extreme climates. Therefore, care must be taken to relieve them from dangerous conditions.

Then, work stress questionnaire is used to assess their mental stress at work. It uses 1–4 scale to evaluate (i.e. yes, yes rather than often, no seldom, no never) (Table 4.13).

It is found that construction site workers were more stressed compared to mining workers. Among 204 construction workers, 137 workers ticked on yes, and 63 on yes rather than often, and 3 workers said no seldom and 1 person said no. Similarly, for mining, 144 workers, 107 workers reported for yes and rest 37 as no.

Worker's name Measurement by Mason Date 2/10/2021

Observer's Assessment

Back

A When performing the task, is the back
(select worse case situation)
A1 Almost neutral?
A2 Moderately flexed or twisted or side bent?
A3 ✓ Excessively flexed or twisted or side bent?

B Select ONLY ONE of the two following task options:

EITHER

For seated or standing stationary tasks. Does the back remain in a static position most of the time?
B1 No
B2 ✓ Yes

OR

For lifting, pushing/pulling and carrying tasks (i.e. moving a load). Is the movement of the back
B3 Infrequent (around 3 times per minute or less)?
B4 ✓ Frequent (around 8 times per minute)?
B5 Very frequent (around 12 times per minute or more)?

Shoulder/Arm

C When the task is performed, are the hands
(select worse case situation)
C1 ✓ At or below waist height?
C2 At about chest height?
C3 At or above shoulder height?

D Is the shoulder/arm movement
D1 Infrequent (some intermittent movement)?
D2 ✓ Frequent (regular movement with some pauses)?
D3 Very frequent (almost continuous movement)?

Wrist/Hand

E Is the task performed with
(select worse case situation)
E1 An almost straight wrist?
E2 ✓ A deviated or bent wrist?

F Are similar motion patterns repeated
F1 10 times per minute or less?
F2 11 to 20 times per minute?
F3 ✓ More than 20 times per minute?

Neck

G When performing the task, is the head/neck bent or twisted?
G1 No
G2 ✓ Yes, occasionally
G3 Yes, continuously

Worker's Assessment

Workers

H Is the maximum weight handled MANUALLY BY YOU in this task?
H1 ✓ Light (5 kg or less)
H2 Moderate (6 to 10 kg)
H3 Heavy (11 to 20kg)
H4 Very heavy (more than 20 kg)

J On average, how much time do you spend per day on this task?
J1 Less than 2 hours
J2 2 to 4 hours
J3 ✓ More than 4 hours

K When performing this task, is the maximum force level exerted by one hand?
K1 ✓ Low (e.g. less than 1 kg)
K2 Medium (e.g. 1 to 4 kg)
K3 High (e.g. more than 4 kg)

L Is the visual demand of this task
L1 ✓ Low (almost no need to view fine details)?
*L2 High (need to view some fine details)?
* *If High, please give details in the box below*

M At work do you drive a vehicle for
M1 Less than one hour per day or Never?
M2 ✓ Between 1 and 4 hours per day?
M3 More than 4 hours per day?

N At work do you use vibrating tools for
N1 ✓ Less than one hour per day or Never?
N2 Between 1 and 4 hours per day?
N3 More than 4 hours per day?

P Do you have difficulty keeping up with this work?
P1 Never
P2 ✓ Sometimes
*P3 Often
* *If Often, please give details in the box below*

Q In general, how do you find this job
Q1 Not at all stressful?
Q2 Mildly stressful?
*Q3 ✓ Moderately stressful?
*Q4 Very stressful?
* *If Moderately or Very, please give details in the box below*

* *Additional details for L, P and Q if appropriate*

*** L** ✓

*** P**

*** Q**

Fig. 4.12 QEC questionnaire for dam construction (infrastructure)

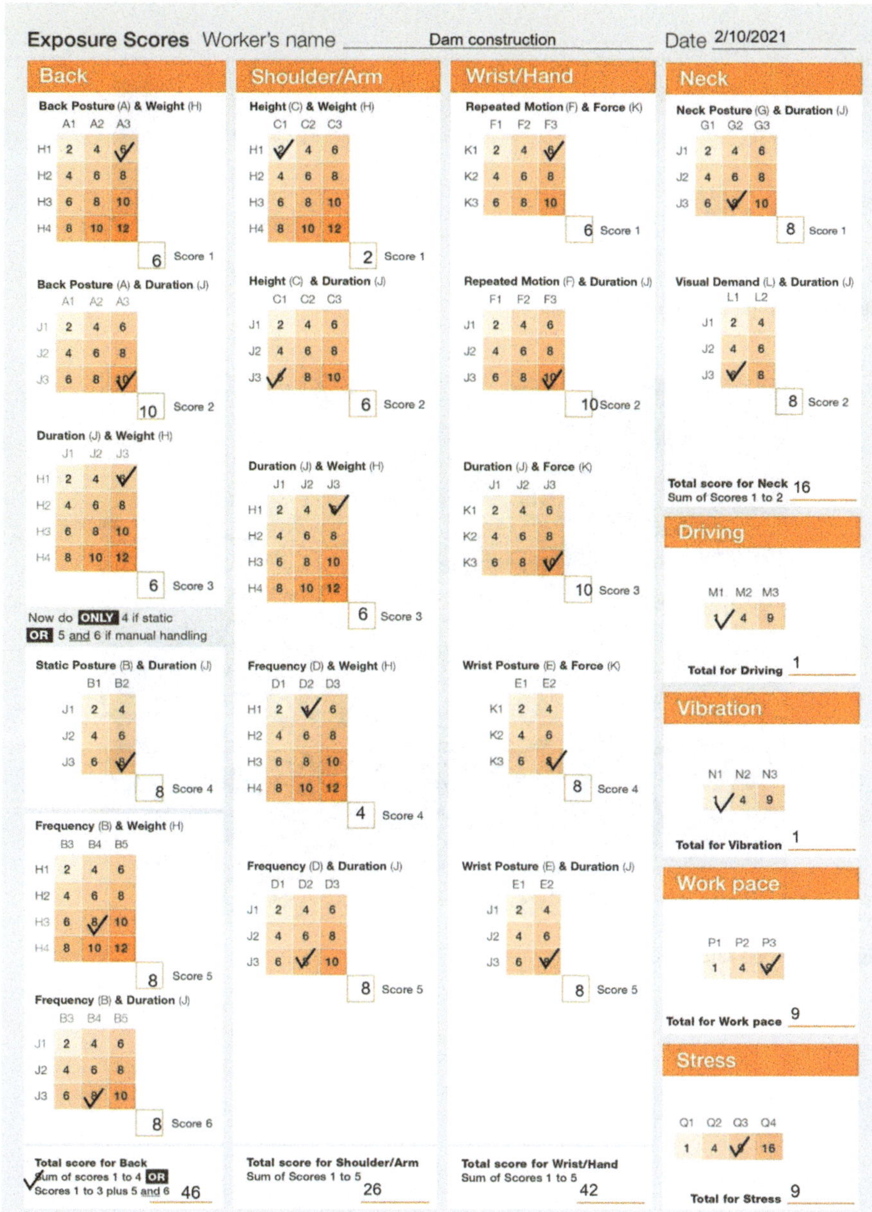

Fig. 4.13 QEC score for dam construction (infrastructure)

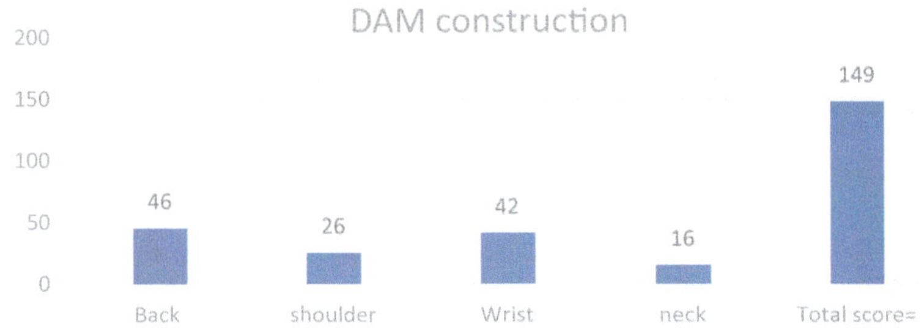

Fig. 4.14 Graph for dam construction

Fig. 4.15 Road safety work

Worker's name Road Work Date

Observer's Assessment

Back

A When performing the task, is the back
(select worse case situation)
- A1 Almost neutral?
- A2 Moderately flexed or twisted or side bent?
- A3 ✓ Excessively flexed or twisted or side bent?

B Select ONLY ONE of the two following task options:

EITHER

For seated or standing stationary tasks. Does the back remain in a static position most of the time?
- B1 No
- B2 ✓ Yes

OR

For lifting, pushing/pulling and carrying tasks (i.e. moving a load). Is the movement of the back
- B3 Infrequent (around 3 times per minute or less)?
- B4 Frequent (around 8 times per minute)?
- B5 ✓ Very frequent (around 12 times per minute or more)?

Shoulder/Arm

C When the task is performed, are the hands
(select worse case situation)
- C1 ✓ At or below waist height?
- C2 At about chest height?
- C3 At or above shoulder height?

D Is the shoulder/arm movement
- D1 Infrequent (some intermittent movement)?
- D2 Frequent (regular movement with some pauses)?
- D3 ✓ Very frequent (almost continuous movement)?

Wrist/Hand

E Is the task performed with
(select worse case situation)
- E1 An almost straight wrist?
- E2 ✓ A deviated or bent wrist?

F Are similar motion patterns repeated
- F1 10 times per minute or less?
- F2 11 to 20 times per minute?
- F3 ✓ More than 20 times per minute?

Neck

G When performing the task, is the head/neck bent or twisted?
- G1 No
- G2 Yes, occasionally
- G3 ✓ Yes, continuously

Worker's Assessment

Workers

H Is the maximum weight handled MANUALLY BY YOU in this task?
- H1 Light (5 kg or less)
- H2 Moderate (6 to 10 kg)
- H3 ✓ Heavy (11 to 20kg)
- H4 Very heavy (more than 20 kg)

J On average, how much time do you spend per day on this task?
- J1 Less than 2 hours
- J2 2 to 4 hours
- J3 ✓ More than 4 hours

K When performing this task, is the maximum force level exerted by one hand?
- K1 Low (e.g. less than 1 kg)
- K2 Medium (e.g. 1 to 4 kg)
- K3 ✓ High (e.g. more than 4 kg)

L Is the visual demand of this task
- L1 Low (almost no need to view fine details)?
- *L2 ✓ High (need to view some fine details)?

* *If High, please give details in the box below*

M At work do you drive a vehicle for
- M1 Less than one hour per day or Never?
- M2 Between 1 and 4 hours per day?
- M3 ✓ More than 4 hours per day?

N At work do you use vibrating tools for
- N1 Less than one hour per day or Never?
- N2 Between 1 and 4 hours per day?
- N3 ✓ More than 4 hours per day?

P Do you have difficulty keeping up with this work?
- P1 Never
- P2 Sometimes
- *P3 ✓ Often

* *If Often, please give details in the box below*

Q In general, how do you find this job
- Q1 Not at all stressful?
- Q2 Mildly stressful?
- *Q3 Moderately stressful?
- *Q4 ✓ Very stressful?

* *If Moderately or Very, please give details in the box below*

* *Additional details for L, P and Q if appropriate*

*L

*P ✓

*Q

Fig. 4.16 Road construction questionnaire

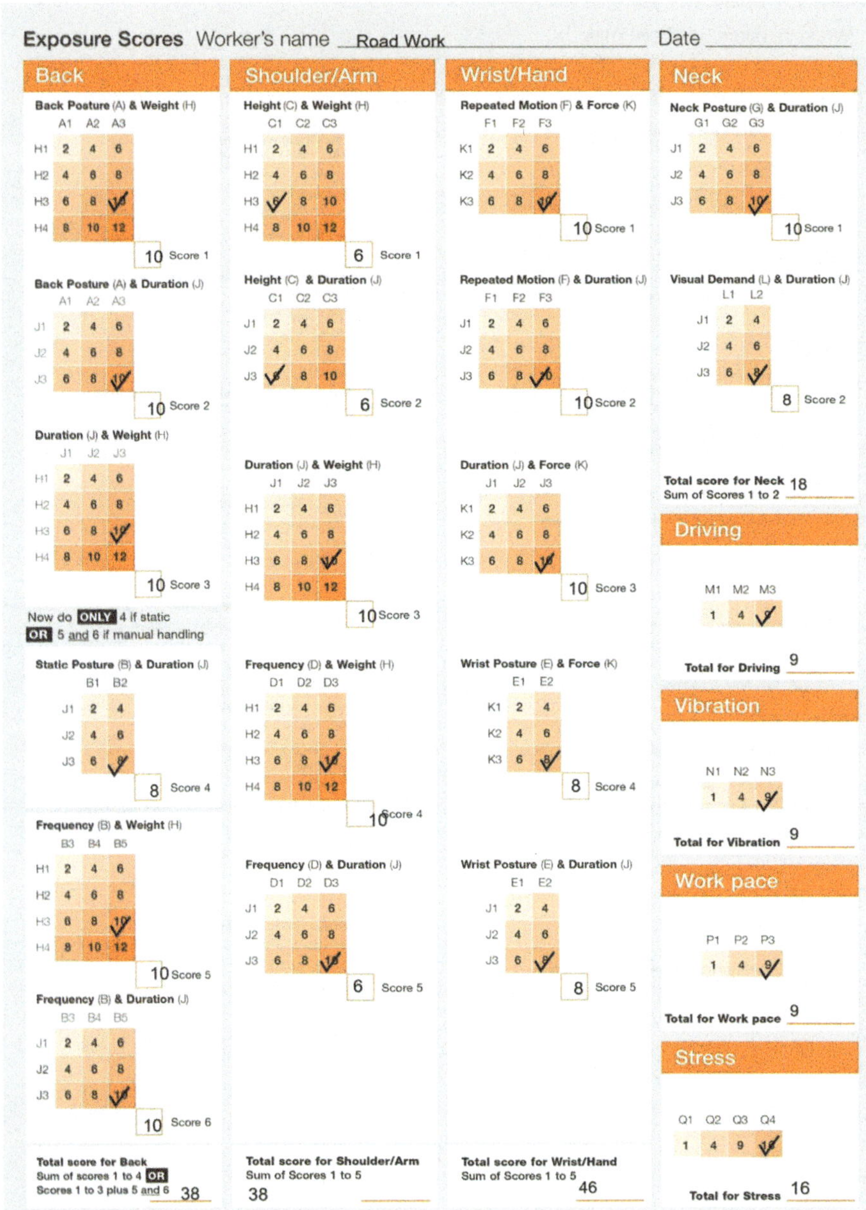

Fig. 4.17 QEC score for road worker

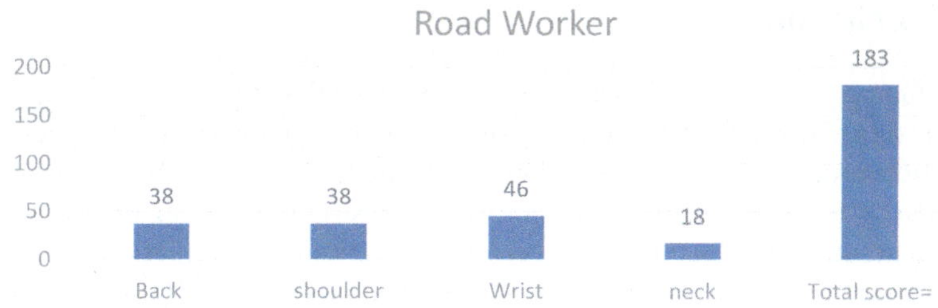

Fig. 4.18 Graph of road work

Table 4.13 Stress question

Work stress	Yes	Yes rather than often	No seldom	No never
Finish your assignments in time				
Do you have any chance of influencing decisions at work?				
Does your boss take into account your opinions?				
Can you control how quickly you work?				
Your workload has it grown?				
Are you feeling work pressure stress full				
Are the objectives for your company clear? Do you find that to be stressful?				
Do you understand whatever tasks you're Work duties comprise				
Do you know the maker of choices affecting your location of employment				
Exist any disputes at work				
Do you participate in any disputes at work				
Has your boss taken any action to resolve the conflicts				
Do you demand a lot of yourself at work	.			
Do you frequently become absorbed in your work				
Do you prefer working after office time				
Even when you have a lot of work to complete, do you find it difficult to set a time limit for each assignment				

4.7 Conclusion

The risk factors for construction site workers are found and prioritized such that the system design requirements of successful sustainable factors can be suggested for construction projects. In this paper, the ARAS method followed by factor analysis is carried out to prioritize the risk factors in construction. After that, ergonomic risk is the greatest risk factor for concern for all types of construction sectors after chemical hazards. To investigate more on ergonomic risk factors, QEC software was used. By analysing some images, the adverse effect on health due to the construction environment and work process is clarified. Similarly, WASPAS method is used to prioritize mining workers' mental stress. For both construction and mining workers work stress is conducted, and it was found that it is found that construction site workers were more stressed compared to mining workers.

References

Agumba, J., & Haupt, T. (2008). Perceptions of construction health and safety performance improvements enablers. In *Proceedings of third built environment conference, Cape Town South Africa.* ASOCSA 2008–2068.

Ajayi, O., & HwDID, W. D. (2012). Dynamics of health and safety in Nigeria's construction industry: Construction worker's dilemma. In G. Nani, R. K. Nkum, E. Awere, E. Kissi, & E. Bamfo-Agyei (Eds.), In *Proceedings of 1st Applied Research on Conference in Africa (ARCA) Conference*, Elmina, Ghana, pp. 430–441.

Albert, A., Hallowell, M. R., & Kleiner, B. M. (2014). Enhancing construction hazard recognition and communication with energy-based cognitive mnemonics and safety meeting maturity model: Multiple baseline study. *Journal of Construction Engineering and Management, 140*(2), 04013042.

Basu, N., Clarke, E., Green, A., Calys-Tagoe, B., Chan, L., Dzodzomenyo, M., Fobil, J., Long, R., Neitzel, R., Obiri, S., Odei, S., Ovadje, L., Quansah, R., Rajaee, M., & Wilson, M. (2015). Integrated assessment of artisanal and small-scale gold mining in Ghana-part 1: Human health review. *International Journal of Environmental Research and Public Health, 12*, 5143–5176.

Bauerle, T., Dugdale, Z., & Poplin Tim Bauerle, G. (2018). Mineworker fatigue: A review of what we know and future decisions. *Mining Engineering, 70*, 33–40.

Bhandari, S., & Hallowell, M. R. (2017). Emotional engagement in safety training: Impact of naturalistic injury simulations on the emotional state of construction workers. *Journal of Construction Engineering and Management, 143*(12), 04017090.

Bhandari, S., Hallowell, M. R., & Correll, J. (2019). Making construction safety training interesting: A field-based quasi-experiment to test the relationship between emotional arousal and situational interest among adult learners. *Safety Science, 117*, 58–70.

Brown, J. P., Martin, D., Nagaria, Z., Verceles, A. C., Jobe, S. L., & Wickwire, E. M. (2020). Mental health consequences of shift work: An updated review. *Current Psychiatry Reports, 22*, 1–7.

Caldwell, J. A., Caldwell, J. L., Thompson, L. A., & Lieberman, H. R. (2019). Fatigue and its management in the workplace. *Neuroscience and Biobehavioral Reviews, 96*, 272–289.

Carlisle, K. N., & Parker, A. W. (2014). Psychological distress and pain reporting in Australian coal miners. *Safety and Health at Work, 5*, 203–209.

Deng, M., Wu, F., Wang, J., & Sun, L. (2017). Musculoskeletal disorders, personality traits, psychological distress, and accident proneness of Chinese coal miners. *Work, 57*, 441–449.

Etuknwa, A., Daniels, K., & Eib, C. (2019). Sustainable return to work: A systematic review focusing on personal and social factors. *Journal of Occupational Rehabilitation, 29*, 679–700.

Ferguson, S. A., Paech, G. M., Dorrian, J., Roach, G. D., & Jay, S. M. (2011). Performance on a simple response time task: Is sleep or work more important for miners? *Applied Ergonomics, 42*, 210–213.

Garbarino, S., Guglielmi, O., Sanna, A., Mancardi, G. L., & Magnavita, N. (2016). Sleep disordered breathing risk of occupational accidents in workers with obstructive sleep apnea: Systematic review and meta-analysis. *Sleep, 39*, 1211–1218.

Golabchi, A., Han, S., Seo, J., Han, S., Lee, S., et al. (2015). An automated biomechanical simulation approach to ergonomic job analysis for workplace design. *Journal of Construction Engineering and Management, 141*, 04015020.

Hung, Y.-H., Winchester, W. W., Smith-Jackson, T. L., Kleiner, B. M., Babski-Reeves, K. L., & Mills, T. H. (2013). Identifying fall-protection training needs for residential roofing subcontractors. *Applied Ergonomics, 44*(3), 372–380.

James, C., Tynan, R., Roach, D., Leigh, L., Oldmeadow, C., Rahman, M., & Kelly, B. (2018). Correlates of psychological distress among workers in the mining industry in remote Australia: Evidence from a multi-site cross-sectional survey. *PLoS ONE, 13*, 1–17.

Jeelani, I., Albert, A., Azcvcdo, R., & Jaselskis, E. J. (2017a). Development and testing of a personalized hazard-recognition training intervention. *Journal of Construction Engineering and Management, 143*(5).

Jeelani, I., Han, K., & Albert, A. (2017b). Development of immersive personalized training environment for construction workers. *ASCE International Workshop on Computing in Civil Engineering, 2017*, 407–415.

Kebrit, D., & Rani, S. (2013). Assessment of work-related musculoskeletal disorders: Causes and prevention. *J Res Sci Tech, 2*, 8.

Loewenson, R. (1999). Assessment of the health impact of occupational risk in Africa: Current situation and Methodological issues. *Epidemiol, 10*, 632–639.

Nakua, E. K., Owusu-Dabo, E., Newton, S., Adofo, K., Otupiri, E., Donkor, P., & Mock, Ch. (2019). Occupational injury burden among gold miners in Ghana. *International Journal of Injury Control and Safety Promotion, 26*, 329–335.

Paech, G. M., Jay, S. M., Lamond, N., Roach, G. D., & Ferguson, S. A. (2010). The effects of different roster schedules on sleep in miners. *Applied Ergonomics, 41*, 600–606.

Pelders, J., & Nelson, G. (2019). Contributors to fatigue at a platinum smelter in South Africa. *Journal of the Southern African Institute of Mining Metallurgy, 119*, 313–319.

Pizarro, J. M., & Fuenzalida, F. A. (2021). Mental health in mine workers: A literature review. *Industrial Health, 59*(6), 343–370.

Rwamamara, R., Lagerqvist, O., Olofsson, T., & Johansson, B. (2007). Best practices for the prevention of work-related musculoskeletal disorders in the construction industry. *Journal Construction Management and Engineering ASCE* 1–21.

Satapathy, S. (2021). Work place discomfort and risk factors for construction site workers. *International Journal of System Assurance Engineering and Management*. https://doi.org/10.1007/s13198-021-01322-5

Schneider, S. P. (2001). Musculoskeletal injuries in construction: A review of the literature. *Applied Occupational and Environmental Hygiene, 16*, 1056–1064.

Vedder, J., & Carey, E. (2005). A multi-level systems approach for the development of tools, equipment and work process for the construction industry. *Work Science and Ergonomics*, 1–20.

Wang, H. H., Zhang, Z. J., Tan, Q. R., Yin, H., Chen, Y. C., Wang, H. N., Zhang, R. G., Wang, Z. Z., Guo, L., Tang, L. H., & Li, L. J. (2010). Psychopathological, biological, and neuroimaging characterization of posttraumatic stress disorder in survivors of a severe coalmining disaster in China. *Journal of Psychiatric Research, 44*, 385–392.

Yu, H., Chen, H., & Long, R. (2017). Mental fatigue, cognitive bias and safety paradox in chinese coal mines. *Resources Policy, 52*, 165–172.

Zavadskas, E. K., Stević, Z., Tanackov, I., & Prentkovskis, O. (2018). A Novel Multicriteria Approach – Rough Step-Wise Weight Assessment Ratio Analysis Method (R-SWARA) and Its Application in Logistics, *Studies in Informatics and Control*, ISSN 1220-1766, vol. *27*(1), pp. 97–106.

Zhao, Y., Richardson, A., Poyser, C., Butterworth, P., Strazdins, L., & Leach, L. S. (2019). Shift work and mental health: A systematic review and meta-analysis. *International Archives of Occupational and Environmental Health, 92*, 763–793.

Chapter 5
Designing a Framework to Reduce the Mental Workload and Improve the Mental Health of Workers Engaged in Animal Farming

Abstract Some percentage of the farming community are dependent on livestock and animal farming. For healthy animal farming, proper care is essential for animals; same way, farmers engaged in animal farming must use protective dresses and equipment to keep themselves safe from many diseases. Air pollution, unhealthy atmosphere, and unhygienic conditions in animal farming create skin and respiratory health effects on farmers. For taking care of animals, the farmers have to work long hours and perform repetitive work. MSDs and posture problems create major health problems among animal farmers. Sometimes, with lots of care, animals die from some weather-related chronic diseases, so the farmers have to bear a lot of financial crises. Health issues, antigenic atmosphere, heavy workload, social pressure, and financial problems are the main causes of mental stress among animal farmers. So the improvement of work environment will benefit both farmer and animals health. Hence an effort is taken to design a framework which can improve the work environment for improving mental health of workers in animal farming.

Keywords Animal farming · Health issues · Mental health · Designing framework

5.1 Introduction

Animal farming is also called as livestock farming, and it is one kind of agrifarming where animals/livestocks were taken care for milk, egg, and meat. Cattle farming, fish farming, poultry farming, and bee farming are included in livestock farming. Livestock farming is a stressful job as the farmer has to look after the animals, fight poverty and diseases, and improve productivity. The animal farmers, like dairy farmers/cattle farmers, have a main issue which is pasture or land shortages for grazing, cattle diseases, theft of cattle, emotional attachment to animals, and conflicts. But in the case of fish farming, poultry farming, and bee farming, requirement of space, diseases, and a lot of care are the most important requirements. FAO (2018) has investigated that animal farmers in Africa were suffering with problems like spreading uncontrollable animal diseases, natural disasters like drought, and pasture

S. Satapathy et al., *Occupational Health Safety Factors and Their Impact on the Mental Health of Workers*, New Perspectives in Behavioral & Health Sciences,
https://doi.org/10.1007/978-981-99-7619-5_5

land battles. The animal protein and animal products are in high demand as it is the main part of food for human race. Padhy (2018) has explored that maintaining farm with adverse climatic condition, natural disaster, and with fluctuating demand is the main tension for farmer. Tseren (2018) have written that unresolved and uncontrollable problems like climate change are the main headache among farmers, which increases mental pressure. Kolstrup et al. (2013) have found that farmer usually loss their livestock in natural calamities and in mentally stress. As per the International Labour Organization (ILO) (2016), workplace stress is the main cause of mental illness and psychological stress and reduction of productivity. From FAO (2017), it is found that the loss of livestock affects production levels. Mottet et al. (2018) have explained about the increasing demand for livestock products. McLeod (2011) by seeing the demand for animal products has predicted that meat and egg consumption will increase by 73% and 58%, respectively, by the year 2050. Rosegrant et al. (2009) have written that animal protein consumption is also increased in Latin America and the Caribbean. As per FAO (2014) fish and aquatic protein demand has also increased all over the world. (OSHA, 2014) has announced that the injury rate of animal farmers is 6.7% more than agriculture farmers and 5.5% more than the crop production farmers.

5.2 Methodology

To study the mental wellness of animal farmers, a case study is conducted by designing a standard questionnaire using literature review and expert suggestion. The experts are academicians, research scholars, animal doctors, psychiatrists, animal farmers, etc. From the discussion below, 19 points found considered as the major factors of mental sickness among animal farmers of India, South Africa, Nepal, Mexico, etc.

1. Work stress is more as farmer has to take care of animals (ILO, 2016).
2. Pressure due to outbreaks of diseases of animals (Burdick Sanchez et al., 2017; Carroll et al., 2017).
3. Lack of attractive policies and financial attention (FAO, 2009).
4. Insurance coverage for animals is much less (FAO, 2009).
5. Less grazing lands, seasonal, and nutrition of animal requirements (Caton et al., 2020; Devendra and Leng, 2011; Hassen et al., 2010).
6. Livestock products lack transparency, uncertain, and underdeveloped.
7. Poor access to an organized market and huge market pressure (FAO, 2017).
8. Isolation in workplace.
9. Lack of advanced technology to make livestock farming smooth and comfortable.
10. Greenhouse gas emissions (Llonch et al., 2017).
11. Performance of animals and trans-generational in effect (Laporta et al., 2020).
12. Environmental effects, droughts, and natural calamities (FAO, 2018).

13. Emotional attachment to animals (FAO, 2018).
14. Fear of theft of animals (FAO, 2018).
15. Conflicts among farmers (Hassen et al., 2010).
16. Staying in unhygienic atmosphere may spread infection from animals.
17. Loss of animals (Carroll et al., 2017).
18. Lack of medical/veterinary facilities for animals (Hassen et al., 2010).
19. Injuries caused by animals (Hassen et al., 2010).

5.3 Results and Discussion

To reduce the mental stress of animal farmers, a system design frame work is designed by Quality function Deployment. In Quality function Deployment Table 5.1 shows HOQ, the relation between customer requirements and design requirements. Fargnoli (2018) has applied the Quality Function Deployment (QFD) technique and assessed how specific tasks may relate to certain hazards, which in turn are linked to certain event, and after all to define which prevention activities/protection measures may be taken against such events. Yazdani et al. (2016) have studied customer attitudes into account in the supplier evaluation process. Chan and Wu (2005) described a high-quality home including the following stages.

1. **Consumer needs (WHAT)**

QFD begins by consumers (Griffin 1992) after all consumers' needs have been recorded; similar needs are collected in groups and written on a sympathy diagram.

2. **Important mass of the consumer**

In order to recognize the great importance of consumer requirements, consumers are surveyed to indicate the importance of each WHAT using grading scales.

3. **Design requirements (HOW)**

Based on literature analysis, customer requirements and design requirements *(HOW)* are determined.

4. **Matrix of the relationships between WHAT and HOW**

In this manual, the data and characters assigned to QFD use 0.8 for long [0], 0.6 for sensitive [⊙], 0.4 for bad [Δ], and 0.2 for very bad [•].

5. **Score rate for HOWs**

Score equity means "how much" the design needs. At this time, based on literature and discussions with farmers, score rate was created for the customer's specific design requirements.

6. **Separate qualification of design needs**

Table 5.1 Shows final ranking by QFD

	Initial rating design requirements	Revised rating	Normalized rating	Rank
S1	43.140	36.52	0.774877997	8
S2	56.0	12.10	0.256736686	
S3	59.45	47.42	1.00	1 (1st)
S4	58.13	34.19	0.725440272	9
S5	55.71	10.34	0.219393168	18
S6	53.69	47.13	0.909531843	3 (3rd)
S7	53.76	41.09	0.8718	4
S8	49.58	39.36	0.8351	6
S9	51.47	40.69	0.8633	5
S10	48.46	27.57	0.584977721	11
S11	94.7	75.86	0.606195629	10
S12	53.20	42.36	0.98932	2 (2nd)
S13	48.12	38.29	0.812433694	7
S14	54.65	10.13	0.214937407	19
S15	55.25	13.52	0.286866115	14
S16	54.23	15.35	0.325694886	13
S17	46.56	18.46	0.39168258	12
S18	51.14	9.84	0.208784214	20
S19	58.45	11.34	0.240611076	17
S20	53.62	13.37	0.283683429	15
S21	55.23	11.556	0.245194144	16

Finally, based on the following calculations, a separate assessment was developed for the design requirements of the learning ability workspace:

Separate classification of the design requirement $= \sum_{j}^{n} A_{ij} X_j$.

HOQ consists of these basic components, as described below.

Consumer needs (WHAT): A list of needs based on expert feedback.

Design requirements (HOW): A typical design of applicable and predictable facilities that are essential to accomplish WHAT.

Design matrix (left matrix): Provides information about the consumers seen in the survey and contains relative demand status.

Relationship matrix (central matrix): They are used to recognize the relationship between design requirements and consumer requirements and apply appropriate sign and use characters or numbers to explain. Completing this part of the matrix requires discussion.

$$\text{Consume revaluation} = Z_i + \frac{1}{n-1}\left(\sum B_{ij} Z_j\right)$$

where B_{ij} = ith initial customers rating and Z_j indicates the relationships between needs and consumer's quality, respectively.

where $B_{ij} = i$th initial rating of the customers and Z_j indicates the relationships between the needs and the rating of the consumers.

$n =$ the number of consumer demand.

$$B_{ij} = \left[B_{1ij}, B_{2ij}, \ldots, B_{nij}\right]$$

The separate classification for each design requirements is obtained from the central matrix using the following relationship as in the equation:

$$\text{Individual qualification of design requirements} = \sum_{j}^{n} A_{ij} X_j$$

A_{ij} and X_j represent the comparison position of the ith feature and the jth consumer's demand in the correlation matrix or the jth customers demand position (consumer's core).

$n =$ the number of customer requirements.

A_{ij} and X_j represent the comparison position of the ith feature in the correlation matrix with respect to the jth consumer request or the position of the jth consumer request (consumer rating).

$n =$ number of consumers who need.

Design requirements to reduce mental stress are found below.

1. Animals must be kept in a shelter to avoid theft.
2. Water and food must be sufficiently available for animals' good health.
3. Farmers must use personal protective equipment to avoid injury during day-to-day activity.
4. Boots and hand gloves must be used to avoid infection.
5. Cleanliness and hygiene must be taken care.
6. Tracking devices must be used to avoid loss of animals.
7. Regular vaccinations and check-ups must be given to avoid the spreading of diseases.
8. Veterinary doctors must be available when required.
9. Insurance of animals must be done.
10. Availability of grazing land for animals must be sufficient.
11. Animal shelter must be provided during a disaster.
12. Proper land distribution must be done to avoid conflict.

13. Law orders, animal police, and courts must be available to resolve the animal-related conflicts.
14. Animal foods must be provided at a subsidized rate.
15. Proper training and education must be provided to animal farmers to take care of their animals to avoid injuries.
16. Proper and automatic instruments must be provided to farmers to reduce their physical stress in taking care of animals.
17. Vaccinations and medicine alerts must be given to farmers for their animals.
18. Regular check-up and counselling must be provided to farmers to reduce their stress level.
19. Circular economic interventions must be put forth to face the challenges of animal farming.
20. Instead of individual animal farming, group animal farming must be supported to reduce mental stress.
21. Workplaces must be developed to support animal farming and reduce physical stress.

To reduce mental stress, Quality Function Deployment (QFD) is implemented and house of quality (HoQ) is designed as per Fig. 5.1. Table 5.1 shows the ranking of QFD.

From Table 5.1, it is found that farmers must use personal protective equipment to avoid injury during day-to-day activity ranked first, tracking devices must be used to avoid loss of animals ranked second, and proper land distribution must be done

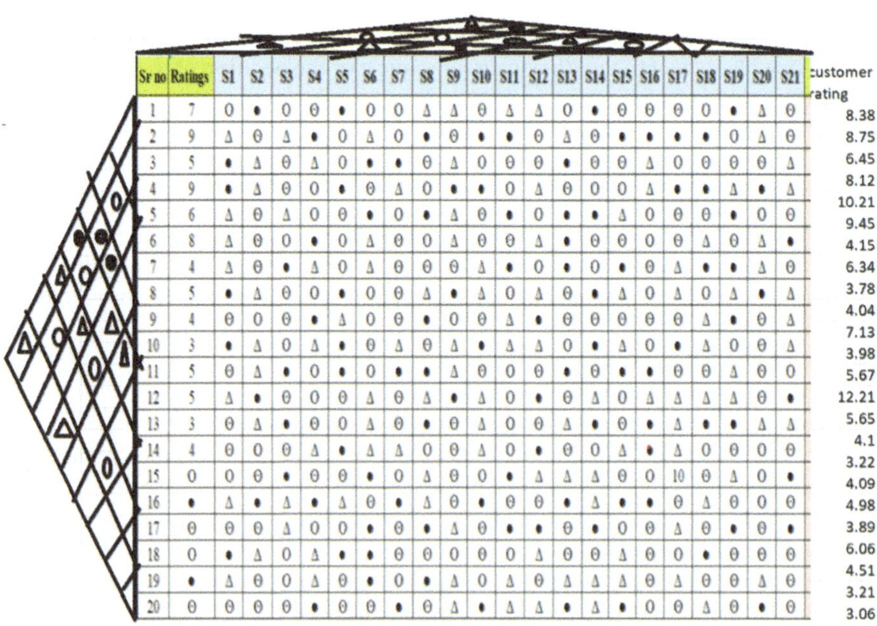

Fig. 5.1 HoQ

to avoid conflict ranked third. Hence, the government must take initiation to frame policies for the safety of animals such that animal farmers can properly take care of animals, and their mental sickness can be reduced.

5.4 Conclusion

Animal farming is a demanding occupation that often exposes farmers to high levels of mental stress. Understanding the key factors that contribute to this stress is crucial in designing an effective framework for its reduction. One significant factor is the financial burden imposed on animal farmers, as they face fluctuating market prices, escalating production costs, and unpredictable weather conditions. Additionally, the physical demands of the job, including long working hours and exposure to hazardous environments, further compound mental strain. The lack of social support networks and limited access to mental health resources are also prevalent challenges faced by animal farmers. Moreover, dealing with disease outbreaks, animal welfare concerns, and strict regulatory requirements adds another layer of pressure. Identifying these key factors provides valuable insights into developing targeted interventions that address the specific needs of animal farmers and alleviate their mental stress effectively. Animal farming is an essential industry that plays a crucial role in our society. However, it is not without its challenges, and one significant concern is the mental stress experienced by animal farmers. The demanding nature of their work, combined with factors such as financial pressures, long working hours, and the emotional attachment to animals, can lead to serious mental health issues. To address this problem effectively, a comprehensive framework must be designed. This framework should focus on three key areas: prevention, support, and education. Prevention strategies may include implementing regular breaks and rest periods for farmers, promoting work-life balance initiatives, and encouraging social support networks within the farming community. Support mechanisms should encompass accessible mental health services tailored specifically for animal farmers. Once the framework for reducing mental stress among animal farmers has been designed, it is crucial to implement and evaluate its effectiveness. The implementation process involves introducing the framework to animal farmers, providing them with necessary training and resources, and ensuring their understanding of its principles. It is important to offer ongoing support during this stage to address any challenges or concerns that may arise. To evaluate the effectiveness of the framework, various metrics can be employed. These may include assessing changes in mental health indicators such as stress levels, anxiety, depression, and overall well-being among animal farmers. Additionally, feedback from farmers themselves should be collected through surveys or interviews to gauge their perception of how the framework has impacted their mental well-being. A comprehensive evaluation will help identify areas where improvements can be made and inform future iterations of the framework.

References

Burdick Sanchez, N. C., Carroll, J. A., Arthington, J. D., & Lancaster, P. A. (2017). Exposure to lipopolysaccharide in utero alters the postnatal metabolic responses in heifers. *Journal of Animal Science, 95*, 5176–5183. https://doi.org/10.2527/jas2016.0885

Carroll, J. A., Burdick Sanchez, N. C., Arthington, J. D., Nelson, C. D., Benjamin, A. L., Korkmaz, F. T., et al. (2017). In utero exposure to LPS alters the postnatal acute-phase response in beef heifers. *Innate Immunity, 23*, 97–108. https://doi.org/10.1177/1753425916678472

Caton, J. S., Crouse, M. S., McLean, K. J., Dahlen, C. R., Ward, A. K., Cushman, R. A., et al. (2020). Maternal periconceptual nutrition, early pregnancy, and developmental outcomes in beef cattle. *Journal of Animal Science, 98*, skaa358. https://doi.org/10.1093/jas/skaa358

Chan, L. K., & Wu, M. L. (2005). A systematic approach to quality function deployment with a full illustrative example. *Omega, 33*(2), 119–139.

Devendra, C., & Leng, R. A. (2011). Invited review—Feed resources for animals in Asia: Issues, strategies for use, intensification and integration for increased productivity. *Asian-Australian Journal of Animal Science, 24*, 303–321.

FAO. (2009). *The State of Food and Agriculture: Livestock in balance*. FAO (August 28, 2014). http://www.fao.org/docrep/012/i0680e/i0680e.pdf

FAO. (2014). *The state of world fisheries and aquaculture: Opportunities and challenges*. FAO.

FAO. (2017). *The future of food and agriculture: Trends and challenges* (p. 180). FAO. Available from http://www.fao.org/publications/card/en/c/d24d2507-41d9-4ec2-a3f8-88a489bfe1ad/

FAO, IFAD, UNICEF, WFP, WHO. (2018). The State of Food Security and Nutrition in the World 2018. In *Building climate resilience for food security and nutrition*. FAO.

Fargnoli, M., Lombardi, M., & Haber, N. (2018). A fuzzy-QFD approach for the enhancement of work equipment safety: A case study in the agriculture sector. *International Journal of Reliability and Safety, 12*(3), 306–326.

Griffin, A. (1992). Evaluating QFD's use in US firms as a process for developing products. *Journal of Product Innovation Management: AN INTERNATIONAL PUBLICATION OF THE PRODUCT DEVELOPMENT & MANAGEMENT ASSOCIATION, 9*(3), 171–187.

Hassen, A., Ebro, A., Kurtu, M., & Treydte, A. C. (2010). Livestock feed resources utilization and management as influenced by altitude in the Central Highlands of Ethiopia. *Livestock Research for Rural Development Newsletter, 22*, 12.

International Labour Organization. (2016). Workplace stress: A collective challenge. In *World day for safety and health at work* (p. 57). ILO.

Kolstrup, C. L., Kallioniemi, M., Lundqvist, P., Kymäläinen, H., & Stallones, L. (2013). International perspectives on psychosocial working conditions, mental health, and stress of dairy farm operators. *Journal of Agromedicine, 18*(3), 244–255.

Laporta, J., Ferreira, F. C., Ouellet, V., Dado-Senn, B., Almeida, A. K., De Vries, A., et al. (2020). Late-gestation heat stress impairs daughter and granddaughter lifetime performance. *Journal of Dairy Science, 103*, 7555–7568. https://doi.org/10.3168/jds.2020-18154

Llonch, P., Haskell, M. J., Dewhurst, R. J., & Turner, S. P. (2017). Current available strategies to mitigate greenhouse gas emissions in livestock systems: An animal welfare perspective. *Animal, 11*, 274–284. https://doi.org/10.1017/S1751731116001440

McLeod, A. (Ed.). (2011). World livestock 2011: Livestock in food security. FAO (September 25, 2014). http://www.fao.org/docrep/014/i2373e/i2373e.pdf

Mottet, A., Teillard, F., Boettcher, P., De' Besi, G., & Besbes, B. (2018). Review: Domestic herbivores and food security: Current contribution, trends and challenges for a sustainable development. *Animal, 12*, s188–s198. https://doi.org/10.1017/S1751731118002215

OSHA (U.S. Department of Labor Occupational Safety and Health Administration). (2014). *Agricultural operations* (September 3, 2014). https://www.osha.gov/dsg/topics/agriculturaloperations/index.html

Padhy, C. (2018). Stress among farmers and its alleviation. *International Journal Management Technology Engineering, 8*(12), 2882–2887.

Rosegrant, M. W., Fernandez, M., Sinha, A., Alder, J., Ahammad, H., de Fraiture, C., Eickhout, B., Fonseca, J., Huang, J., Koyama, O., Omezzine, A. M., Pingali, P., Ramirez, R., Ringler, C., Robinson, S., Thornton, P., van Vuuren, D., & Yana-Shapiro, H. (2009). Looking into the future for agriculture and AKST (Agricultural Knowledge Science and Technology). In B. D. McIntyre, H. R. Herren, J. Wakhungu, & R. T. Watson (Eds.), *Agriculture at a crossroads* (pp. 307–376). Island Press.

Tseren, B. (2018). Reducing herders' vulnerability to climate change through community-based pastureland management in Mongolia. *Solut Journal, 9*(4). Available from https://www.thesolutionsjournal.com/author/battsetseg-tseren/

Yazdani, M., Hashemkhani Zolfani, S., & Zavadskas, E. K. (2016). New integration of MCDM methods and QFD in the selection of green suppliers. *Journal of Business Economics and Management, 17*(6), 1097–1113.

Chapter 6
Exploring the Mental Pressure of Workers Engaged in White-Collar Jobs

Abstract Occupational stress is one of the most important health hazards in the workplace. It includes physical illness, abuse at workplace, work stress due to long working hours, complex work culture, family problems, etc. These are the main issues faced by maximum employees in white-collar jobs. The white-collar jobs are official jobs with less physical load and more mental pressure. Awkward (continuous sitting posture), long working hours, more mental stress to compete with co-workers, and goal (target)-oriented job detach the person from social life. To reduce stress, employees start drinking and smoking regularly, which will create health diseases and disturb family life and financial crises. Hence, the cause of mental pressure is studied and explored in this chapter, by studying the working postures such that steps can be suggested to improve their mental health.

Keywords Ergonomic · Mental stress · White-collar employees · REBA

6.1 Introduction

In recent years, there has been a noticeable surge in the prevalence of mental pressure among workers engaged in white-collar jobs. These professionals, typically employed in corporate settings, face unique challenges that contribute to their heightened stress levels. One primary factor is the increasing demand for productivity and efficiency in today's highly competitive work environments. The constant need to meet deadlines, achieve targets, and juggle multiple responsibilities can lead to overwhelming mental pressure. Moreover, the nature of white-collar jobs often involves long working hours and minimal breaks, leaving little time for relaxation and recuperation. The incessant use of technology further exacerbates this issue as employees are constantly connected to work even outside office hours. This blurring of boundaries between personal and professional lives adds an additional layer of stress. The mental pressure experienced by workers engaged in white-collar jobs is a complex phenomenon influenced by several factors. One crucial factor is the high level of competition prevalent in these professions. The constant need to outperform peers

S. Satapathy et al., *Occupational Health Safety Factors and Their Impact on the Mental Health of Workers*, New Perspectives in Behavioral & Health Sciences,
https://doi.org/10.1007/978-981-99-7619-5_6

and meet demanding targets creates an atmosphere of intense pressure, leading to elevated stress levels. Moreover, the expectation of long working hours and tight deadlines adds to the mental strain experienced by employees. The fear of failure and job insecurity exacerbate this pressure, as individuals strive to maintain their position in a highly competitive environment. Additionally, technological advancements have significantly impacted workplace dynamics, with employees now being constantly connected through various digital platforms. This 24/7 accessibility blurs work-life boundaries, resulting in increased mental pressure as individuals struggle to find time for personal relaxation and rejuvenation. In the fast-paced and demanding world of white-collar jobs, workers often face significant mental pressure that can have a profound impact on their overall well-being and performance. The incessant deadlines, high workload, and constant need to meet expectations can result in heightened stress levels, leading to various negative consequences. Firstly, the mental pressure experienced by workers can severely affect their well-being.

It may lead to increased anxiety, burnout, and even depression. Physical health issues such as headaches, insomnia, and weakened immune system are also commonly observed among individuals under prolonged mental pressure. Moreover, the adverse effects extend beyond personal well-being and manifest in decreased work performance. Mental pressure impairs concentration and decision-making abilities while hindering creativity and problem-solving skills. This ultimately hampers productivity levels and quality of work output.

(1) Prioritize self-care: Engage in regular exercise, maintain a balanced diet, and ensure sufficient sleep to enhance physical and mental well-being. Taking breaks during working hours can help recharge the mind and reduce stress. (2) Establish work-life boundaries: Set clear limits between work and personal life by avoiding excessive overtime or bringing work-related stress home. Create dedicated spaces for relaxation and leisure activities to foster a healthier work-life balance. (3) Seek social support: Maintain healthy relationships with colleagues, friends, and family members who can provide emotional support. Engaging in open conversations about workplace stressors can help alleviate the burden. (4) Practice mindfulness techniques: Incorporate mindfulness exercises into daily routines to manage stress effectively. Techniques like deep breathing, meditation, or yoga can enhance focus, reduce anxiety levels, and improve overall mental well-being.

Scott and Taylor (1985) have explained the negative relationship between absenteeism and job satisfaction. Arnold and Feldman (1982), O'Driscoll et al. (1992), Stumpf and Hartman (1984) have explored that organizational commitment has a good and positive correlation with job satisfaction. Lazarus and Folkman (1984) have found that potential stressors that individuals may experience depend on how they perceive stress in their minds. However, Nelson and Quick (1985) found that due to the unique job stresses that women confront (career barriers, lower wages, discrimination, and the dynamic between family duties and profession), women report more occupational stress than men. The work system (WS) is an all-encompassing term that takes into account all pertinent factors and facets of working (employee, task, tool, organization, and work environment) (ISO, 2004). As Hatch and Cunliffe (2013) concluded, social interactions, attitudes, and feelings at work are impacted by organizational distinctions and changes, including management, technologies, and technology. Memish et al. (2017) and Deloitte (2017) have enlightened that workplace stress is the main cause of mental stress. Martens et al. (1999), Kim et al. (2013), Kato et al. (2014), and Kuroda and Yamamoto (2016) have explored positive relation between working hours and worker's mental stress.

6.2 Research Methodology

To explore causes of stress in the workplace for white-collar professionals, a standard questionnaire is designed with extensive literature review and expert (academia and industry experts) suggestions and circulated among white-collar professionals, like professors and administrative personnel of universities, software professionals, bankers, and power and utility companies employees. A 5-point Likert scale was used to collect data (1 = agree, 2 = somewhat agree, 3 = no opinion, 4 = somewhat disagree, and 5 = disagree). The data was collected through personal contact, telephonic interviews from countries like Mexico, India, Malaysia, Papua New Guinea, Bangladesh, etc. The selected white-collar professionals have 5–20 years of experience and have been working in the same sector more than 5 years and not suffering with any kind of chronic diseases. A total of 111 data was collected for 17 questions (Figs. 6.1, 6.2 and Table 6.1).

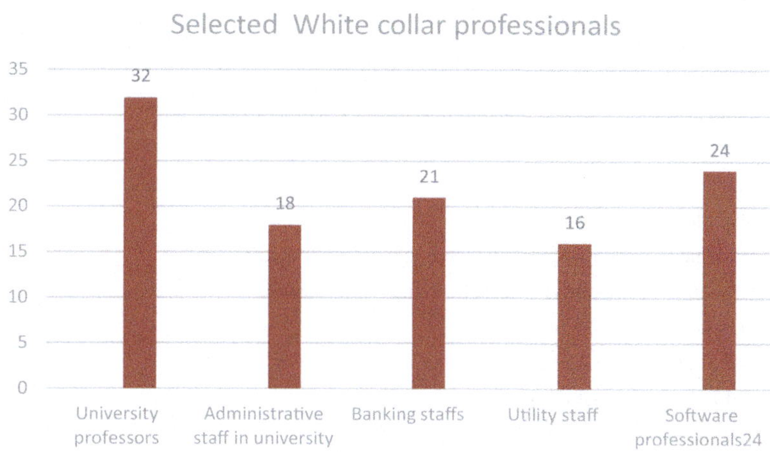

Fig. 6.1 Selected white-collar professionals

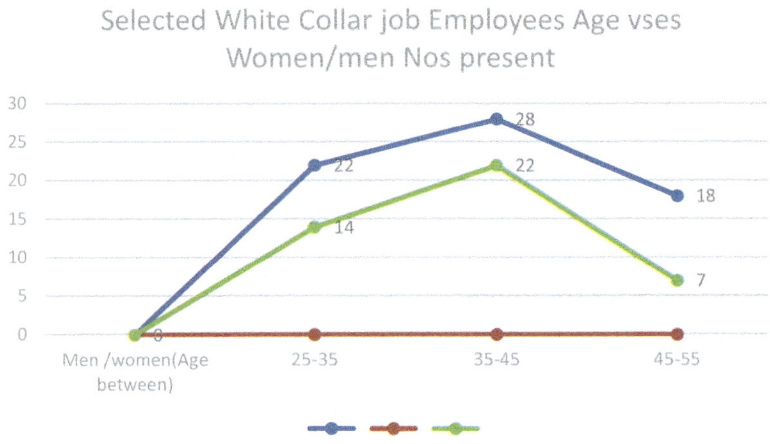

Fig. 6.2 Selected white-collar job employees' age verses women and men nos

Table 6.1 Questionnaire

Sl. no	Question	1	2	3	4	5
1	Lack of physical exercise					
2	Lack of relief from work					
3	Intense supervision and control of workers by managers					
4	Hazardous material risk					
5	Sedentary kind of life					
6	Damage from repetitive motion					
7	Stress on the eyes					
8	Occupational violence					
9	Threats of job loss and outsourcing, whether actual or imagined					
10	Stress at work					
11	Unhealthy indoor air					
12	Gender violence/harassment					
13	Unable to work in advanced technology or work culture					
14	Too much competitive atmosphere and work pressure					
15	Lack of job satisfaction					
16	Musculoskeletal disorder and discomfort posture of working					
17	Monetary dissatisfaction					
18	Dissatisfaction with granting leave					

6.3 Results and Discussion

To find the collected perception of white-collar professionals, the average values of collected data were taken with the help of Likert scale. From Table 6.2, it was found that maximum people support MSDs, repetitive work, etc. which were the main cause of stress in the workplace. Hence, ergonomic and psychological analysis was done to explore the cause of mental stress. The different body postures needed, energetic exertion, the sort of movement or action, repetition, and difficulty of taking are all assessed using the REBA method (Rapid Entire Body Assessment).

Figures 6.3 and 6.4 show the REBA analysis and REBA result score of university professors, and Fig. 6.5 shows the result as corrective action required. Similarly, Figs. 6.6 and 6.7 represent the scores of software professionals and recommends corrective action required. Figures 6.8 and 6.9 show the REBA analysis scores of banking staff, Figs. 6.10 and 6.11 show REBA score for utility staff, and Figs. 6.12 and 6.13 show administrative staff. Among them, utility staff are in great danger; as per the REBA score, immediate action is required. For administrative staff, no action is required, and corrective action is required for bank employees.

Then psychological stress is measured by the PSS scale to measure mental stress.

Table 6.2 Average score of collected value

Sl. no	Question	Percentage
1	Lack of physical exercise	18.91
2	Lack of relief from work	43.24
3	Intense supervision and control of workers by managers	75.67
4	Hazardous material risk	22.52
5	Sedentary kind of life	10.81
6	Damage from repetitive motion	80.18
7	Stress on the eyes	51.35
8	Occupational violence or conflict	13.51
9	Threats of job loss and outsourcing, whether actual or imagined	50.45
10	Stress at work	74.77
11	Unhealthy indoor air	0.081
12	Gender violence/harassment	17.11
13	Unable to work in advanced technology or work culture	64.86
14	Too much competitive atmosphere and work pressure	73.87
15	Lack of job satisfaction	45.94
16	Musculoskeletal disorder and discomfort posture of working	88.28
17	Monetary dissatisfaction	63.93
18	Dissatisfaction with granting leave	43.24

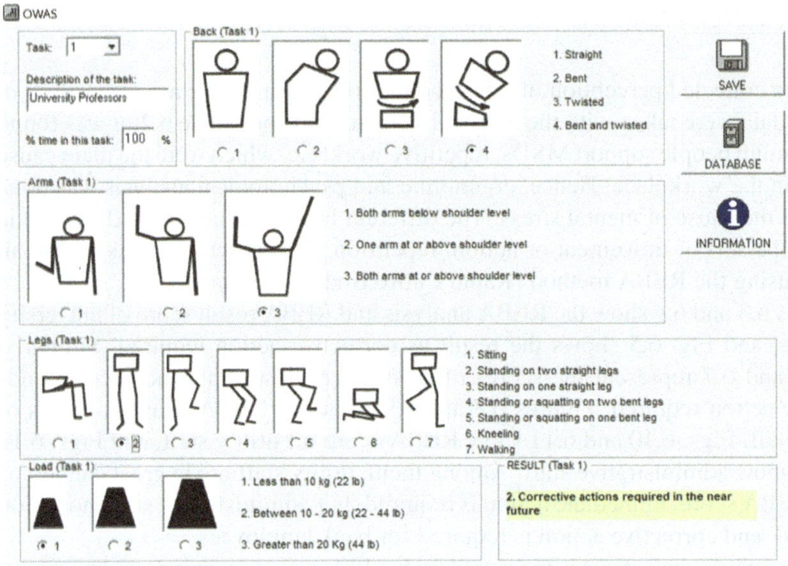

Fig. 6.3 University professors

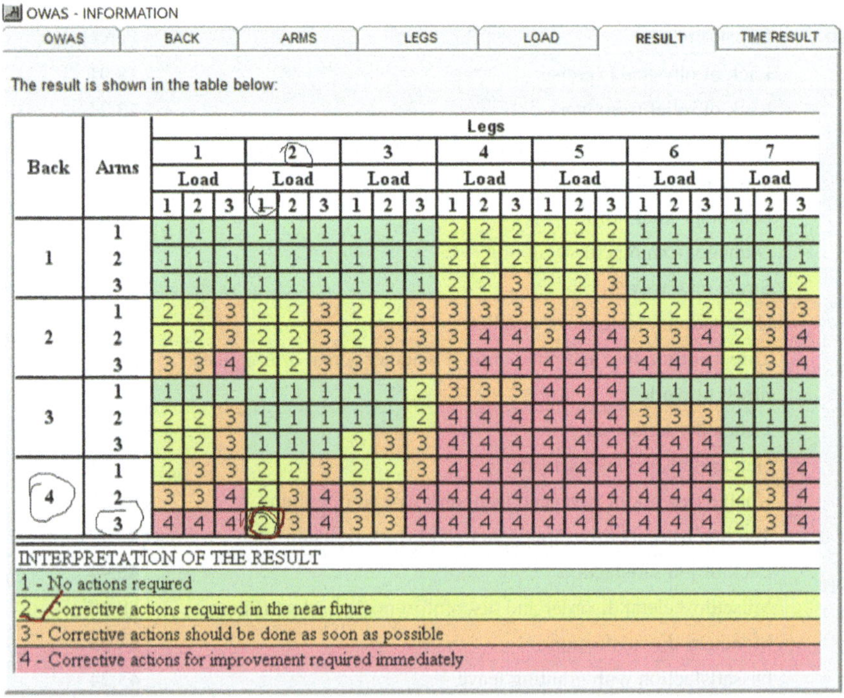

Back	Arms	Legs																				
		1			2			3			4			5			6			7		
		Load			Load			Load			Load			Load			Load			Load		
		1	2	3	1	2	3	1	2	3	1	2	3	1	2	3	1	2	3	1	2	3
1	1	1	1	1	1	1	1	1	1	1	2	2	2	2	2	2	1	1	1	1	1	1
	2	1	1	1	1	1	1	1	1	1	2	2	2	2	2	2	1	1	1	1	1	1
	3	1	1	1	1	1	1	1	1	1	2	2	3	2	2	3	1	1	1	1	1	2
2	1	2	2	3	2	2	3	2	2	3	3	3	3	3	3	3	2	2	2	2	3	3
	2	2	2	3	2	2	3	2	3	3	3	4	4	3	4	4	3	3	4	2	3	4
	3	3	3	4	2	2	3	3	3	3	3	4	4	4	4	4	4	4	4	2	3	4
3	1	1	1	1	1	1	1	1	1	2	3	3	3	4	4	4	1	1	1	1	1	1
	2	2	2	3	1	1	1	1	1	2	4	4	4	4	4	4	3	3	3	1	1	1
	3	2	2	3	1	1	1	2	3	3	4	4	4	4	4	4	4	4	4	1	1	1
4	1	2	3	3	2	2	3	2	2	3	4	4	4	4	4	4	4	4	4	2	3	4
	2	3	3	4	2	3	4	3	3	4	4	4	4	4	4	4	4	4	4	2	3	4
	3	4	4	4	2	3	4	3	3	4	4	4	4	4	4	4	4	4	4	2	3	4

INTERPRETATION OF THE RESULT
1 - No actions required
2 - Corrective actions required in the near future
3 - Corrective actions should be done as soon as possible
4 - Corrective actions for improvement required immediately

Fig. 6.4 Result score for university professors

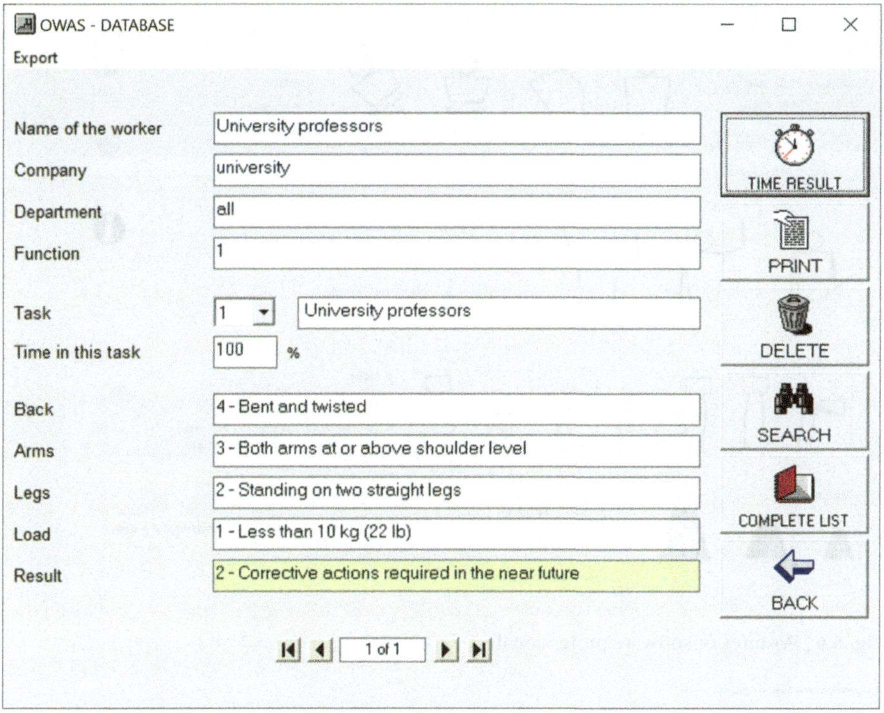

Fig. 6.5 Result of university professors

PSS is a psychological tool used to measure the stress level of a person by a set of questions and with personal questions interaction. The PSS scale consists of 10 numbers of questions, about previous experience obtained by a person. Table 6.3 PSS scale is used to measure psychological or mental stress of all professionals selected for research on the scale 0—never, 1—almost never, 2—sometimes, 3—fairly often, and 4—very often.

After collecting the PSS score, steps are used to calculate PSS score in Table 6.4.

- The collected PSS scores of 4, 5, 7, and 8 were reversed.
  Example. $0 = 4, 1 = 3, 2 = 2, 3 = 1, 4 = 0$.
- Total scores of 10 of PSS questions were added, including reverse scores of 4, 5, 7, and 8 questions.
- When the total score lies between 0 and 40, the stress is very high.
- The total score level between 0 and 13 is low stress.
- And a total score value of 14–26 is moderate stress.
- Scores of between 27 and 40 is high perceived stress.

From Table 6.4, it is found that utility officers and engineers' scores are very high, which means they are under mental stress, and from previous ergonomic REBA score results, it is revealed that these utility staff are also in danger and need immediate

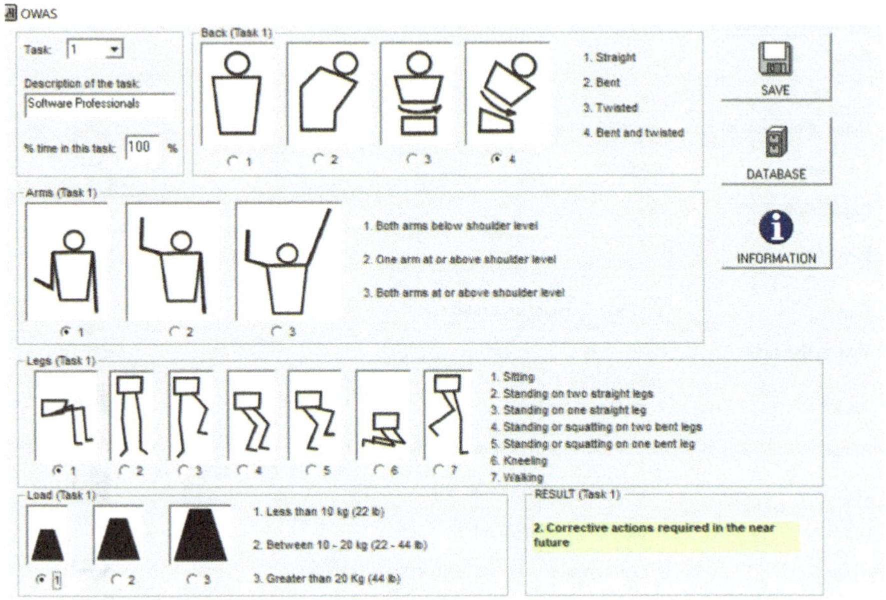

Fig. 6.6 Postures of software professionals

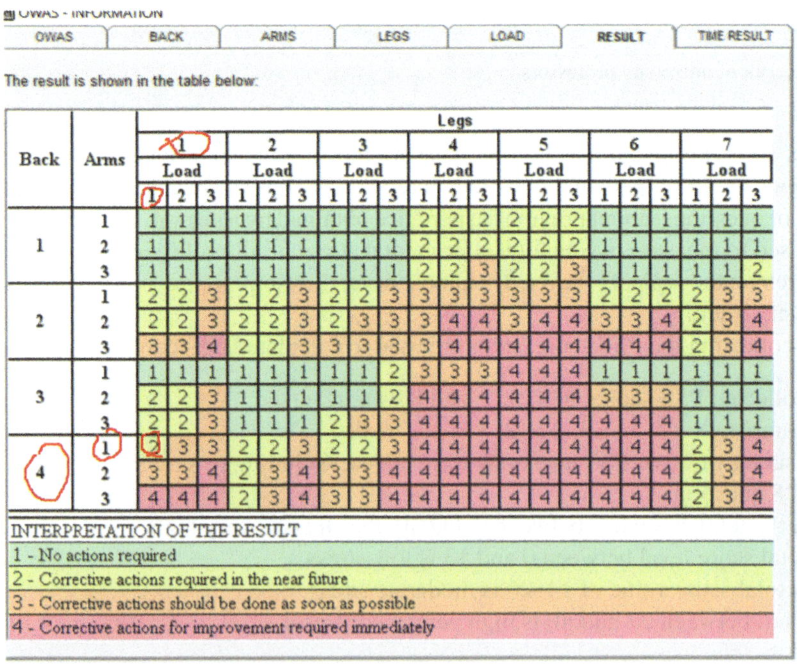

OWAS - INFORMATION

OWAS | BACK | ARMS | LEGS | LOAD | RESULT | TIME RESULT

The result is shown in the table below:

Back	Arms	Legs 1			2			3			4			5			6			7		
		Load			Load			Load			Load			Load			Load			Load		
		1	2	3	1	2	3	1	2	3	1	2	3	1	2	3	1	2	3	1	2	3
1	1	1	1	1	1	1	1	1	1	1	2	2	2	2	2	2	1	1	1	1	1	1
	2	1	1	1	1	1	1	1	1	1	2	2	2	2	2	2	1	1	1	1	1	1
	3	1	1	1	1	1	1	1	1	1	2	2	3	2	2	3	1	1	1	1	1	2
2	1	2	2	3	2	2	3	2	2	3	3	3	3	3	3	3	2	2	2	2	3	3
	2	2	2	3	2	2	3	2	3	3	3	4	4	3	4	4	3	3	4	2	3	4
	3	3	3	4	2	2	3	3	3	3	3	4	4	4	4	4	4	4	4	2	3	4
3	1	1	1	1	1	1	1	1	1	2	3	3	3	4	4	4	1	1	1	1	1	1
	2	2	2	3	1	1	1	1	1	2	4	4	4	4	4	4	3	3	3	1	1	1
	3	2	2	3	1	1	1	2	3	3	4	4	4	4	4	4	4	4	4	1	1	1
4	1	2	3	3	2	2	3	2	2	3	4	4	4	4	4	4	4	4	4	2	3	4
	2	3	3	4	2	3	4	3	3	4	4	4	4	4	4	4	4	4	4	2	3	4
	3	4	4	4	2	3	4	3	3	4	4	4	4	4	4	4	4	4	4	2	3	4

INTERPRETATION OF THE RESULT

1 - No actions required

2 - Corrective actions required in the near future

3 - Corrective actions should be done as soon as possible

4 - Corrective actions for improvement required immediately

Fig. 6.7 Result score of software professionals

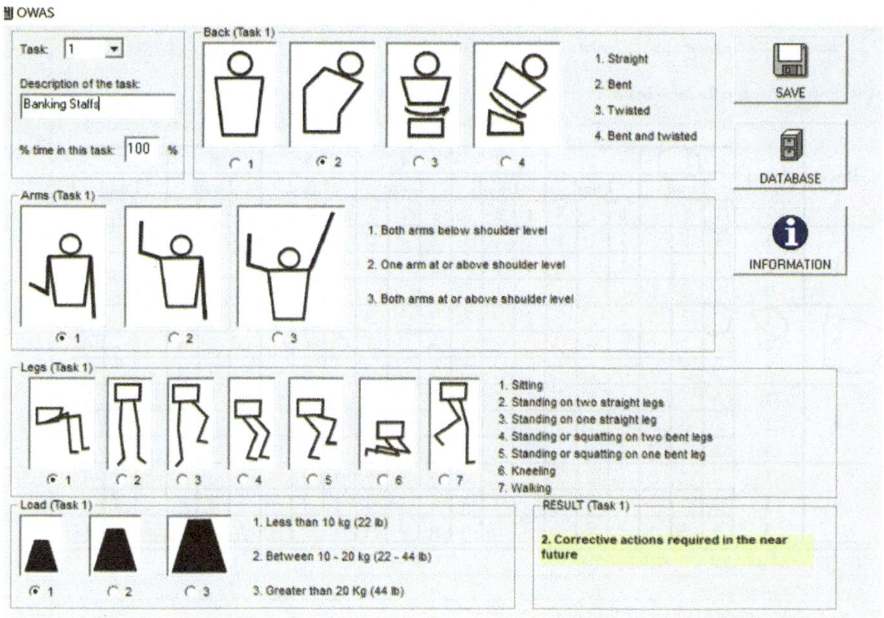

Fig. 6.8 Banking staff

action. It shows that physical work stress also highly impacts mental stress. The next PSS score is for university professors, and if related to their ergonomic REBA score, it also suggests corrective action.

OWAS - INFORMATION

OWAS | BACK | ARMS | LEGS | LOAD | RESULT | TIME RESULT

The result is shown in the table below:

Back	Arms	Legs 1 Load 1	1 Load 2	1 Load 3	2 Load 1	2 Load 2	2 Load 3	3 Load 1	3 Load 2	3 Load 3	4 Load 1	4 Load 2	4 Load 3	5 Load 1	5 Load 2	5 Load 3	6 Load 1	6 Load 2	6 Load 3	7 Load 1	7 Load 2	7 Load 3
1	1	1	1	1	1	1	1	1	1	1	2	2	2	2	2	2	1	1	1	1	1	1
	2	1	1	1	1	1	1	1	1	1	2	2	2	2	2	2	1	1	1	1	1	1
	3	1	1	1	1	1	1	1	1	1	2	2	3	2	2	3	1	1	1	1	1	2
2	1	2	2	3	2	2	3	2	2	3	3	3	3	3	3	3	2	2	2	2	3	3
	2	2	2	3	2	2	3	2	3	3	3	4	4	3	4	4	3	3	4	2	3	4
	3	3	3	4	2	2	3	3	3	3	3	4	4	4	4	4	4	4	4	2	3	4
3	1	1	1	1	1	1	1	1	1	2	3	3	3	4	4	4	1	1	1	1	1	1
	2	2	2	3	1	1	1	1	1	2	4	4	4	4	4	4	3	3	3	1	1	1
	3	2	2	3	1	1	1	2	3	3	4	4	4	4	4	4	4	4	4	1	1	1
4	1	2	3	3	2	2	3	2	2	3	4	4	4	4	4	4	4	4	4	2	3	4
	2	3	3	4	2	3	4	3	3	4	4	4	4	4	4	4	4	4	4	2	3	4
	3	4	4	4	2	3	4	3	3	4	4	4	4	4	4	4	4	4	4	2	3	4

INTERPRETATION OF THE RESULT

1 - No actions required

2 - Corrective actions required in the near future

3 - Corrective actions should be done as soon as possible

4 - Corrective actions for improvement required immediately

Fig. 6.9 Result for banking staff

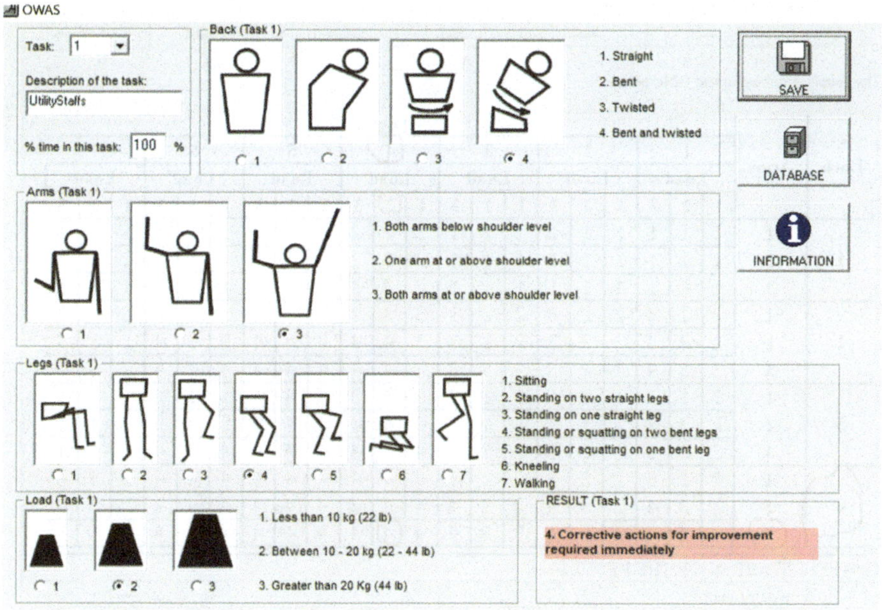

Fig. 6.10 Utility staff

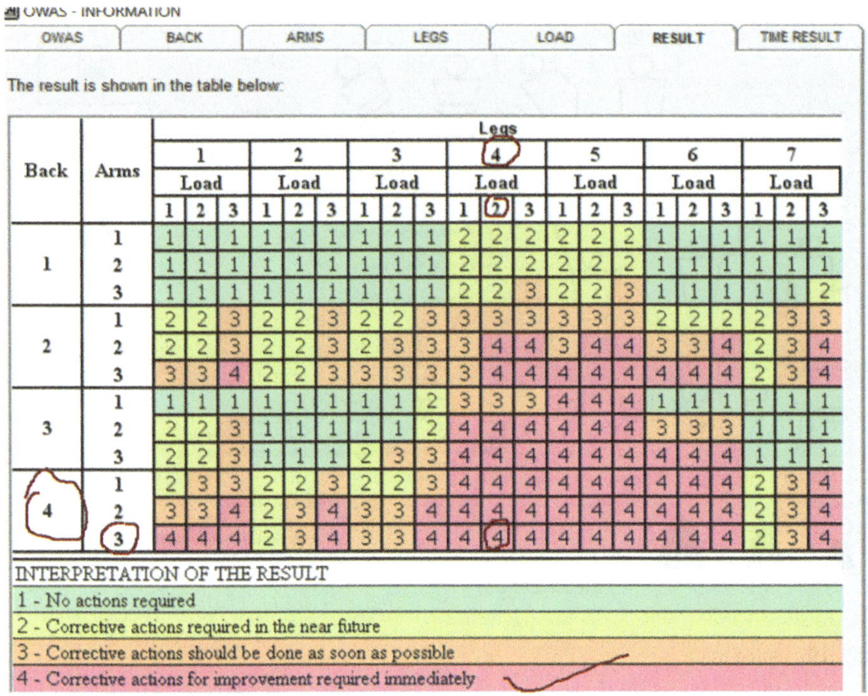

OWAS - INFORMATION

OWAS | BACK | ARMS | LEGS | LOAD | RESULT | TIME RESULT

The result is shown in the table below:

Back	Arms	Legs 1 Load 1	Legs 1 Load 2	Legs 1 Load 3	Legs 2 Load 1	Legs 2 Load 2	Legs 2 Load 3	Legs 3 Load 1	Legs 3 Load 2	Legs 3 Load 3	Legs 4 Load 1	Legs 4 Load 2	Legs 4 Load 3	Legs 5 Load 1	Legs 5 Load 2	Legs 5 Load 3	Legs 6 Load 1	Legs 6 Load 2	Legs 6 Load 3	Legs 7 Load 1	Legs 7 Load 2	Legs 7 Load 3
1	1	1	1	1	1	1	1	1	1	1	2	2	2	2	2	2	1	1	1	1	1	1
	2	1	1	1	1	1	1	1	1	1	2	2	2	2	2	2	1	1	1	1	1	1
	3	1	1	1	1	1	1	1	1	1	2	2	3	2	2	3	1	1	1	1	1	2
2	1	2	2	3	2	2	3	2	2	3	3	3	3	3	3	3	2	2	2	2	3	3
	2	2	2	3	2	2	3	2	3	3	3	4	4	3	4	4	3	3	4	2	3	4
	3	3	3	4	2	2	3	3	3	3	3	4	4	4	4	4	4	4	4	2	3	4
3	1	1	1	1	1	1	1	1	1	2	3	3	3	4	4	4	1	1	1	1	1	1
	2	2	2	3	1	1	1	1	1	2	4	4	4	4	4	4	3	3	3	1	1	1
	3	2	2	3	1	1	1	2	3	3	4	4	4	4	4	4	4	4	4	1	1	1
4	1	2	3	3	2	2	3	2	2	3	4	4	4	4	4	4	4	4	4	2	3	4
	2	3	3	4	2	3	4	3	3	4	4	4	4	4	4	4	4	4	4	2	3	4
	3	4	4	4	2	3	4	3	3	4	4	4	4	4	4	4	4	4	4	2	3	4

INTERPRETATION OF THE RESULT

1 - No actions required

2 - Corrective actions required in the near future

3 - Corrective actions should be done as soon as possible

4 - Corrective actions for improvement required immediately

Fig. 6.11 Result for utility staff

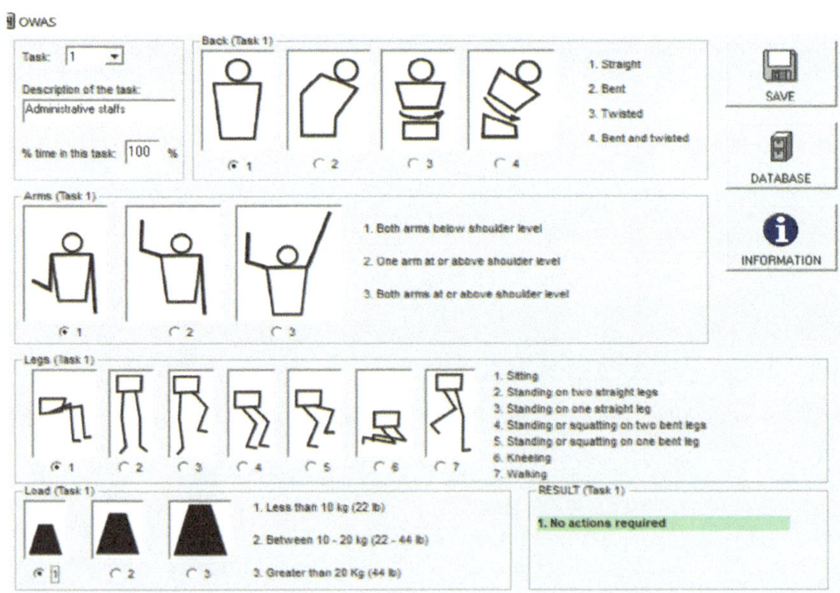

Fig. 6.12 Administrative staff

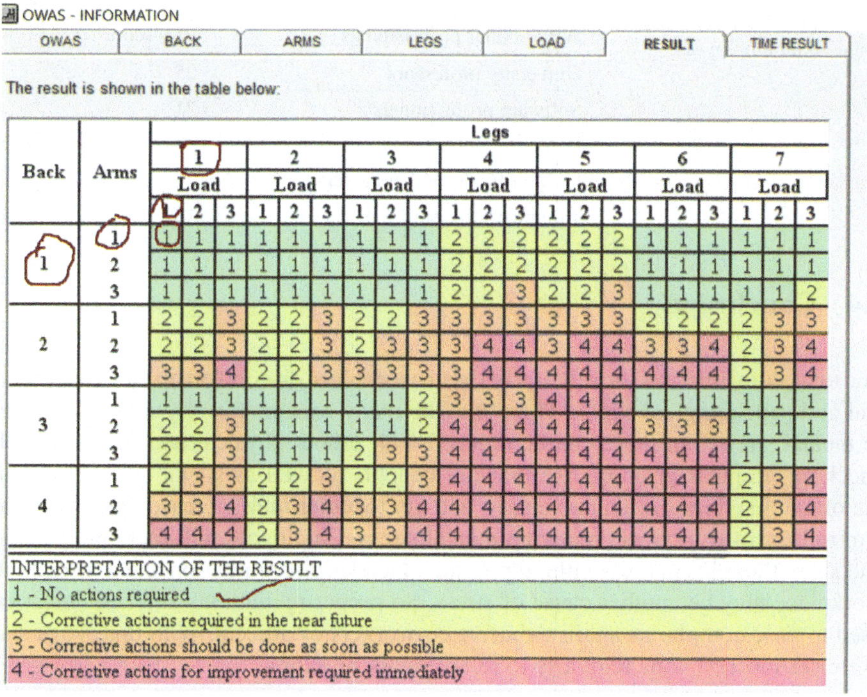

Back	Arms	Legs																				
		1			2			3			4			5			6			7		
		Load			Load			Load			Load			Load			Load			Load		
		1	2	3	1	2	3	1	2	3	1	2	3	1	2	3	1	2	3	1	2	3
1	1	1	1	1	1	1	1	1	1	1	2	2	2	2	2	2	1	1	1	1	1	1
	2	1	1	1	1	1	1	1	1	1	2	2	2	2	2	2	1	1	1	1	1	1
	3	1	1	1	1	1	1	1	1	1	2	2	3	2	2	3	1	1	1	1	1	2
2	1	2	2	3	2	2	3	2	2	3	3	3	3	3	3	3	2	2	2	2	3	3
	2	2	2	3	2	2	3	2	3	3	3	4	4	3	4	4	3	3	4	2	3	4
	3	3	3	4	2	2	3	3	3	3	3	4	4	4	4	4	4	4	4	2	3	4
3	1	1	1	1	1	1	1	1	1	2	3	3	3	4	4	4	1	1	1	1	1	1
	2	2	2	3	1	1	1	1	1	2	4	4	4	4	4	4	3	3	3	1	1	1
	3	2	2	3	1	1	1	2	3	3	4	4	4	4	4	4	4	4	4	1	1	1
4	1	2	3	3	2	2	3	2	2	3	4	4	4	4	4	4	4	4	4	2	3	4
	2	3	3	4	2	3	4	3	3	4	4	4	4	4	4	4	4	4	4	2	3	4
	3	4	4	4	2	3	4	3	3	4	4	4	4	4	4	4	4	4	4	2	3	4

INTERPRETATION OF THE RESULT
1 - No actions required
2 - Corrective actions required in the near future
3 - Corrective actions should be done as soon as possible
4 - Corrective actions for improvement required immediately

Fig. 6.13 Result for administrative staff

Table 6.3 PSS scale

PSS Question	00	11	22	33	44
How many times have you become agitated due to an unexpected event in the past month?					
How many times over the past month have you felt powerless to influence the significant events in your life?					
How often have you felt anxious and stressed over the past month?					
How frequently did you feel assured in your capacity to manage your personal issues in the past month?					
How often did you feel like things were going your way in the past month?					
How frequently did you feel you could not handle everything you had to do in the past month?					
How frequently have you been able to manage irritants in your life over the past month?					
How frequently did you feel in control of the situation in the past month?					
How often did things happen that were out of your control in the past month that made you angry?					
How often did you feel that challenges were increasing so quickly in the past month?					

Table 6.4 PSS scores for white-collar employees

White-collar professionals	PSS score
University professors	25
Software professionals	21
Bankers	18
Utility officers and engineers	38
Administrative staff	10

6.4 Conclusion

The total study imposes the relation between workplace discomfort on workers' physical and psychological stress. There may be many reasons for physical discomfort or mental stress, but these can be reduced with proper physical and mental health check-up. Regular promotions, financial benefits as well as social celebrations in the office, like birthdays, anniversary, and get together may increase the conducive atmosphere in workplace, reducing mental stress. Employees will feel comfortable and share thoughts openly without pressure. Gender discrimination and abuse in the workplace may be another cause of stress. So proper regulations and cells must be used to raise complaints against abusive co-workers or officers. With that, yoga and exercises must be done regularly to relieve work pressure.

References

Arnold, H. J., & Feldman, D. C. (1982). A multivariate analysis of the determinants of job turnover. *Journal of Applied Psychology, 67*, 350–360.

Deloitte. (2017). *At a tipping point? Workplace mental health and wellbeing.*

Hatch, M. J., & Cunliffe, A. N. (2013). *Organization theory, modern, symbolic, and postmodern perspectives* (3rd ed.). Oxford University Press.

ISO. (2004). *International and European Standard. EN ISO 6385: Ergonomic principles in the design of work systems.* International Organization for Standardization.

Kato, R., Haruyama, Y., Endo, M., Tsutsumi, A., & Muto, T. (2014). Heavy overtime work and depressive disorder among male workers. *Occupational Medicine, 64*(8), 622–628 (*Environment and Health*, 515–520).

Kim, I., Kim, H., Lim, S., Lee, M., Bahk, J., June, K. J., Kim, S., & Chang, W. J. (2013). Working hours and depressive symptomatology among full-time employees: Results from the fourth Korean National Health and Nutrition Examination Survey (2007—2009). *Scandinavian Journal of Work.*

Kuroda, S., & Yamamoto, I. (2016). *Workers' mental health, long work hours, and workplace management: Evidence from workers' longitudinal data in Japan.* RIETI.

Lazarus, R. S., & Folkman, S. (1984). *Stress appraisal and coping.* Springer-Verlag.

Martens, M. F. J., Nijhuis, F. J., Van Boxtel, M. P., & Knottnerus, J. A. (1999). Flexible work schedules and mental and physical health. A study of a working population with non-traditional working hours. *Journal of Organizational Behavior: The International Journal of Industrial, Occupational and Organizational Psychology and Behavior, 20*(1), 35–46.

Memish, K., Martin, A., Bartlett, L., Dawkins, S., & Sanderson, K. (2017). Workplace mental health: An international review of guidelines. *Preventive Medicine, 101*, 213–222.

Nelson, D. L., & Quick, J. C. (1985). Professional women: Are distress and disease inevitable?. *Academy of Management Review, 10*(2), 206–218.

O'Driscoll, M. P., Ilgen, D. R., & Hildreth, K. (1992). Time devoted to job and off-job activities, interrole conflict and affective experiences. *Journal of Applied Psychology, 77*, 272–279.

Scott, K. D., & Taylor, G. S. (1985). An examination of conflicting findings on the relationship between job satisfaction and absenteeism: A meta-analysis. *Academy of Management Journal, 28*, 599–612.

Stumpf, S. A., & Hartman, K. (1984). Individual exploration to organizational commitment or withdrawal. *Academy of Management Journal, 27*, 308–329.

Chapter 7
Finding Mental Stress of Agriwomen Farmers Engaged with Heavy Farm Work

Abstract In the farming community, many women participate actively in agriculture and related business regardless of their age. Their role is uncountable and critical in farming. Irrespective of land quality, type of land, and weather conditions, women farmers perform a variety of agricultural operations in all parts of the world. To meet everyday household needs, rural women are responsible for the combined management and utilization of varied natural resources. Furthermore, the rights of women farmers will be critical in increasing agricultural productivity. Women farmers are under greater pressure and mental stress due to heavy physical activity in farming as well as household work. Stress levels might rise over time as a result of economic and family stresses. Hence, in this chapter, an effort is taken to find physical and mental stress in farming.

Keywords Farming · Physical stress · Mental stress · Women farmers

7.1 Introduction

The health and wellness of female farmers are a complex and current issue all over the world. Women agrifarmers have to take on the dual responsibility of taking care of their families and also helping their male relatives in farming. Women farmers suffer from mental and physical stress due to a heavy workload and household responsibilities. Still, in many developing countries, male members of the family are the legal inheritors of ancestral land property. Women members of farming families help their fathers and brothers with farming work from childhood, but as per the old dividend rule of properties and lands, male children have their paternal or ancestral land. Although girls or female children help, they have no right to their paternal land. After marriage, these girls or female farmers help their husbands, their in-law families, and later help their sons in field in farming job. Still, the female farmers have no claim on the land. This system proceeds from generation to generation. In many cases, the male members have to go to towns or urban areas to earn more money, and the female members have to stay in rural areas and take care of farming and household

S. Satapathy et al., *Occupational Health Safety Factors and Their Impact on the Mental Health of Workers*, New Perspectives in Behavioral & Health Sciences,
https://doi.org/10.1007/978-981-99-7619-5_7

work. The female farmers also neglect their health issues and work for their families. Due to heavy physical stress, female farmers suffer from mental stress. Agricultural activities include a lot of strenuous physical labour. Women farmers have to work in hot summers, severe rain, and frigid winters. Women farmers have to perform a few farming activities, like ploughing, harvesting, sowing, weeding, and seeding, and they have to take care of their farm animals without resting. Some farming actions are carried out manually, while others are carried out with the assistance of machines. However, practically all jobs are repetitive by nature and require a lot of physical effort. Due to the heavy workload and field jobs in adverse climatic conditions, women farmers experience a lot of discomfort in body parts, like their knees, backbones, shoulders, etc. Uncomfortable body postures and work-related injuries have a negative impact on mental health. Mental or psychological stress has been identified as a significant factor that can influence an individual's performance when doing a variety of hard tasks. Women farmers have to take care of their families and farm simultaneously with physical and mental discomfort. Uncomfortable positions often lead to injuries and accidents for the workers, which not only decreases productivity but also increases production costs. An ergonomic posture analysis is therefore essential, in order to identify, alleviate, and prevent uncomfortable postures of workers when the workplace design is changed (Chu et al., 2019).

To reduce financial stress for the sake of their families, many women farmers also engage themselves in farming on a wage basis. Findeis (2002a, 2002b) have discussed that in the USA, women farmers' employment increased on a wage basis. Nakajima (1986) and Findeis (2002a, 2002b) have written that, due to an increase in labour costs, women farmers engage themselves in full-time farming. Rosenfeld (1985) done survey and found that in the USA, 37% of farm women work in farms to earn wages. Berkowitz and Perkins (1984) have explored from a survey and path analysis that husband support also plays an important part to keep both balance between work and family of women dairy farmers. Deary et al. (1997) found from a survey among UK farmers that women farmers were more stressed than male farmers, and mixed types and dairy farmers were more stressed and in financial pressure than other types of farmers. Giesen et al. (1989) reported that for women farmers among all kind of stresses like financial stresses, time pressure, work pressure, and mental support from husband, the support from husband is the main cause of their mental well-being. Walker et al. (1986) have reported that among Manitoba farm men and women, main causes of stress are government policies, weather, and volatile market. Derringer and Biddle (2022) have explored that by providing counselling education, stress of farmers can be reduced. Booth and Lloyd (2000) have found that women farmers were more depressed and anxious due to their family problems and physical sickness in the southwest of England than male members of their family. Lobao and Meyer (1995) have shown that farming ladies face more elevated levels of social-mental pressure than men due to their numerous roles played in family and agricultural fields.

7.2 Methodology

To assess stress among women farmers of developing countries like India, Bangladesh, Mexico, and Nepal, a survey is conducted by designing a standard questionnaire. The questionnaire consists of demographic profile like name, age, husband's name, married/unmarried, no. of child, education, income, working hours, the number of years engaged in farming, acres of land owned or farmers engaged on wage basis, etc. In particular, women farmers aged 18–50 and with 10–15 years of farming experience without no chronic diseases are selected for survey. Their working postures were recorded with a camera and analysed by ergonomic software quick exposure check (QEC) to measure physical stress among women farmers and psychological scale. Perceived Stress Scale (PSS) is used to measure mental stress. PSS scores are calculated by inverting collected data. For zero response, 4 is written, and for 1 response, 3 is written, and vice versa for 4 and 3 occurs. For 2 responses, it remains the same. For items 4, 5, 7, and 8, the scale only changes in reverse order, and lastly the summation is done for all scale items in PSS.

7.3 Results and Discussion

To assess the mental stress of women farmers, the total number of 200 women farmers was selected. Among them, 50 farmers were Indian, 50 from Nepal, 50 from Mexico, and the rest 50 from Bangladesh. From the survey, it is found that women farmers are engaged in different types of farming operations, 50% of farmers busy with weeding, 25% with transplanting, 20% with plucking, and rest 5% are engaged in threshing and with other kinds of farming operations. Among (200) women farmers, 22 women aged 20–25 have their own land, 128 women work on their father's, brother's, spouse's, and relatives' land, and 50 work on a daily wage basis. So, after survey and analysis, an ergonomic study is conducted by image and video analysis. It is observed that some female farmers work for 7–8 h daily on a fixed job without change. So for those farmers performing continuously, fixed farming operations in difficult postures are selected for further study. It is found that the female farmers engaged with weeding, plant transplanting, and plucking work doing repetitive job in a constant position. So, those female farmers' images were taken and a quick exposure check (QEC) analysis is done by ErgoFellow software. Figures 7.1, 7.4, and 7.5 show the images of women doing farming jobs like weeding, plucking of vegetables, and paddy transplanting. Figures 7.2 and 7.3 show QEC analysis and QEC score calculation. Table 7.1 shows the QEC score obtained.

QEC is implemented for female farmers engaged in paddy transplantation and also in plucking. Table 7.1 shows that women farmers engaged in weeding operations were at high risk of MSDs compared to other operations. So Perceived Stress Scale (PSS) analysis is conducted for only women farmers engaged with weeding operations to test their mental health condition.

Fig. 7.1 Weeding done by farm women

From Table 7.2, PSS shows that the score for plucking (individual) is 22, which means the women farmer is under moderate stress. Likewise, the PSS score for weeding and transplantation is also calculated in Table 7.3.

It is seen that maximum physical and psychological stress is faced by women farmers in weeding work compared to other farming operations. Weeding means removing unwanted plants from the paddy field. It is a lengthy process. A person has to sit or bend for long time to conduct this operation. It cannot be done in mechanized way as searching and removing weeds is a tactful job. Hence, lengthy working hours and repetitive work are hazardous and create stress physically and mentally. So more research in work pattern is essential.

Recommendation

- Policies may be framed for distribution of 8–10 h jobs to different operations of 2 h such that a person can work only for 2 h in one type of job.
- More people must be engaged to work together to make the work atmosphere lighter.
- Music can be played to make work joyful.
- Policies for work allowances must be framed for refreshment and rest.
- Some kind of small wooden chairs may be provided for a comfortable sitting position.
- Some automated reapers may be programmed to detect weeds and remove them.

Worker's name ______________________ Date __________

Observer's Assessment

Back

A When performing the task, is the back
(select worse case situation)
A1 Almost neutral?
A2 Moderately flexed or twisted or side bent?
A3 Excessively flexed or twisted or side bent?

B Select ONLY ONE of the two following task options:

EITHER

For seated or standing stationary tasks. Does the back remain in a static position most of the time?
B1 No
B2 Yes

OR

For lifting, pushing/pulling and carrying tasks (i.e. moving a load). Is the movement of the back
B3 Infrequent (around 3 times per minute or less)?
B4 Frequent (around 8 times per minute)?
B5 Very frequent (around 12 times per minute or more)?

Shoulder/Arm

C When the task is performed, are the hands
(select worse case situation)
C1 At or below waist height?
C2 At about chest height?
C3 At or above shoulder height?

D Is the shoulder/arm movement
D1 Infrequent (some intermittent movement)?
D2 Frequent (regular movement with some pauses)?
D3 Very frequent (almost continuous movement)?

Wrist/Hand

E Is the task performed with
(select worse case situation)
E1 An almost straight wrist?
E2 A deviated or bent wrist?

F Are similar motion patterns repeated
F1 10 times per minute or less?
F2 11 to 20 times per minute?
F3 More than 20 times per minute?

Neck

G When performing the task, is the head/neck bent or twisted?
G1 No
G2 Yes, occasionally
G3 Yes, continuously

Worker's Assessment

Workers

H Is the maximum weight handled MANUALLY BY YOU in this task?
H1 Light (5 kg or less)
H2 Moderate (6 to 10 kg)
H3 Heavy (11 to 20kg)
H4 Very heavy (more than 20 kg)

J On average, how much time do you spend per day on this task?
J1 Less than 2 hours
J2 2 to 4 hours
J3 More than 4 hours

K When performing this task, is the maximum force level exerted by one hand?
K1 Low (e.g. less than 1 kg)
K2 Medium (e.g. 1 to 4 kg)
K3 High (e.g. more than 4 kg)

L Is the visual demand of this task
L1 Low (almost no need to view fine details)?
•L2 High (need to view some fine details)?
• *If High, please give details in the box below*

M At work do you drive a vehicle for
M1 Less than one hour per day or Never?
M2 Between 1 and 4 hours per day?
M3 More than 4 hours per day?

N At work do you use vibrating tools for
N1 Less than one hour per day or Never?
N2 Between 1 and 4 hours per day?
N3 More than 4 hours per day?

P Do you have difficulty keeping up with this work?
P1 Never
P2 Sometimes
•P3 Often
• *If Often, please give details in the box below*

Q In general, how do you find this job
Q1 Not at all stressful?
Q2 Mildly stressful?
•Q3 Moderately stressful?
•Q4 Very stressful?
• *If Moderately or Very, please give details in the box below*

• *Additional details for L, P and Q if appropriate*

• L

• P

• Q

Fig. 7.2 QEC analysis of weeding

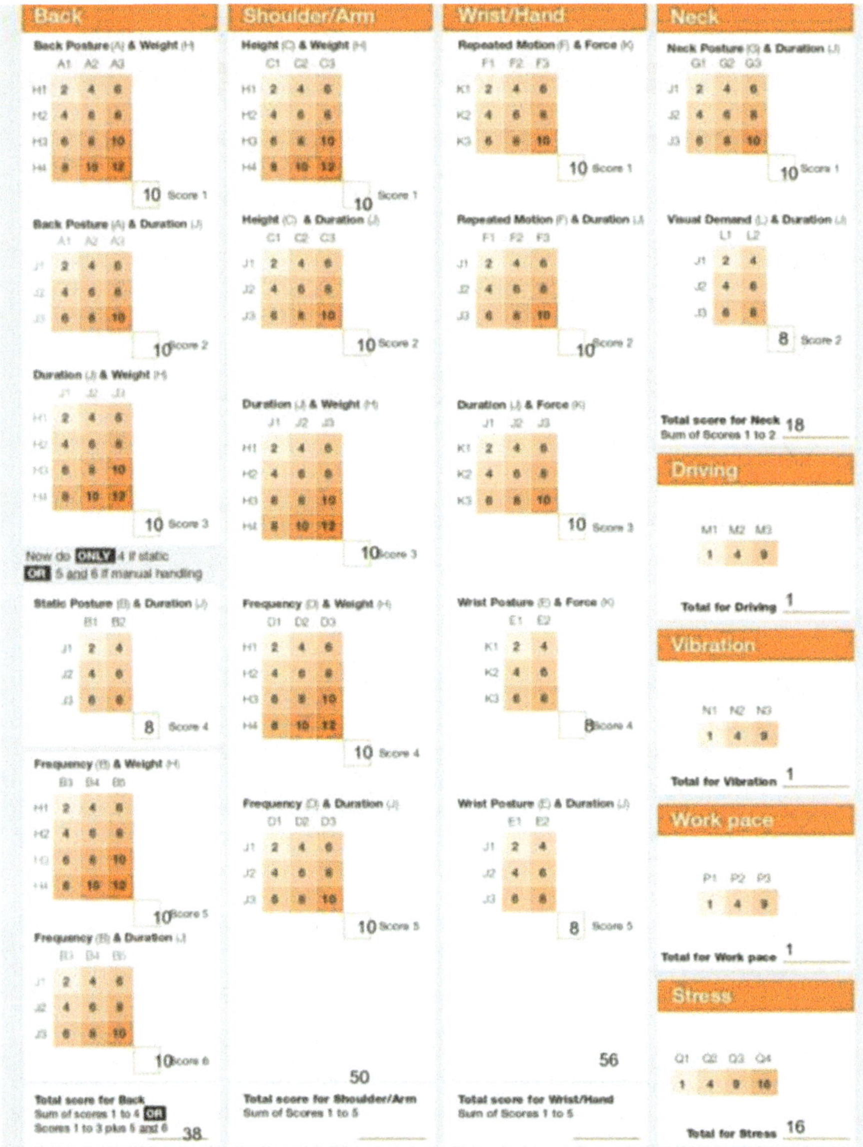

Fig. 7.3 Weeding score calculation

Fig. 7.4 Shows women engaging in a plucking operation

Fig. 7.5 Paddy transplantation

Table 7.1 QEC calculation for weeding, transplantation, and plucking

Sl. No	Total score back	Total score shoulder	Total score wrist/hand	Total score for neck	Total score stress
Weeding	38	50	56	18	16
Transplantation	38	46	48	16	16
plucking	40	46	48	16	16

Table 7.2 Psychological stress scale for plucking (P1)

	0—never	1—almost never	2—sometimes	3—fairly often	4—very often
	4	3	2	1	0
How many times have you become agitated due to an unexpected event in the past month?	4				
How many times over the past month have you felt powerless to influence the significant events in your life?			2		
How often have you felt anxious and stressed over the past month?					0
How frequently did you feel assured in your capacity to manage your personal issues in the past month?				1	
How often did you feel like things were going your way in the past month?		3			
How frequently did you feel you could not handle everything you had to do in the past month?			2		
How frequently have you been able to manage irritants in your life over the past month?	4				

(continued)

Table 7.2 (continued)

	0—never	1—almost never	2—sometimes	3—fairly often	4—very often
How frequently did you feel in control of the situation in the past month?					0
How often did things happen that were out of your control in the past month that made you angry?	4				
How often did you feel that challenges were increasing so quickly in the past month?			2		

Low stress = 0–13, moderate stress = 14–26, and high perceived stress = 27–40.

Table 7.3 PSS total score for women farmer

Total no. of farmers	Total score (individual)	Average score
Weeding (100)	42	45
Transplantation (50)	36	34
Plucking (48)	22	25

7.4 Conclusion

Women farmers contribute to agriculture more than their counterparts. But their contribution is never counted or credited as they are dependent on their male family members. Being uneducated, they are dependent on male members for the necessary paperwork. Therefore, policies, awareness, and education, these three necessary tools, may help women to be independent in farming. This policies also may be helpful to reduce psychological stress among women farmers of India. More training and education of farming and training of using advanced mechanized farming machines may reduce their physical effort and time factor. The women farmers can balance their physical and psychological stress, and the suicidal sickness may be reduced.

References

Berkowitz, A. D., & Perkins, H. W. (1984). Stress among farm women: Work and family as interacting systems. *Journal of Marriage and the Family*, 161–166.

Booth, N. J., & Lloyd, K. (2000). Stress in farmers. *International Journal of Social Psychiatry, 46*(1), 67–73.

Deary, I. J., Willock, J., & McGregor, M. (1997). Stress in farming. *Stress Medicine, 13*(2), 131–136.

Derringer, J. C., & Biddle, M. J. (2022). Potential directions for farm stress research: A systematic review of educational interventions to reduce psychosocial stress among farm and rural populations. *The Journal of Rural Health, 38*(3), 554–573.

Findeis, J. (2002a). Farm Women in the United States. In *Paper presented at the 2002 USDA Ag update forum, February, Washington, DC*.

Findeis, J. L. (2002b). *Subjective equilibrium theory of the farm household: Theory revisited and new directions* (No. 1226-2016-98668).

Giesen, C., Maas, A., & Vriens, M. (1989). Stress among farm women: A structural model approach. *Behavioral Medicine, 15*(2), 53–62.

Lobao, L., & Meyer, K. (1995). Economic decline, gender, and labor flexibility in family-based enterprises: Midwestern farming in the 1980s. *Social Forces, 74*(2), 575 (Chapel Hill).

Nakajima, C. (1986). *Subjective equilibrium theory of the farm household*. Elsevier.

Rosenfeld, R. (1985). *Farm women*. University of North Carolina Press.

Van Chu, T., Thoai, T. Q., An, C. Q., Toai, P. M., Camacho, L. D., & Van Sam, H. (2019). Contribution of forest to rural households' livelihood: evidences from Da river basin in the northwest mountainous region of Vietnam. *Forest and Society, 3*(2), 235–247.

Walker, J. L., Walker, L. S., & MacLennan, P. M. (1986). An informal look at farm stress. *Psychological Reports, 59*(2), 427–430.

Chapter 8
Conclusion with Comparative Analysis of Psychological Stress of Workers with Respect to Gender and Work Type

Abstract Psychological stress is seen as a crucial factor since it might impair people's performance when they attempt to complete difficult jobs at all levels. In fact, completing the task successfully interferes with the task's successful completion when participants are subjected to a higher level of psychological stress that seems unacceptable. One of the most harmful physical and mental reactions at work is stress, which can result from a variety of circumstances. Stress at work may result from increased workload demands and a loss of situational control. In this chapter, a study is carried out to find psychological stress genderwise and jobwise by different types of psychological stress scales like PSS and Holmes and Rahe Stress Scale.

Keywords PSS · Holmes and Rahe stress scale · Workload · Gender type

8.1 Introduction

Mental health of workers plays an important role in life irrespective of gender and job type. There are many reasons for which people suffer from mental stress. The main causes of mental stress may be due to family disturbance, poor health, poverty, job shortage, chronic illness, daily conflicts, and challenges in the workplace, heavy workload, lifestyle imbalance, or disorder. As per job type and job process, physical stress varies, so does mental stress. The mental health of women worker force is different from that of male workers. Mental health is a big and prolonged problem of society. Hence, more research is required to find the root cause of mental stress.

S. Satapathy et al., *Occupational Health Safety Factors and Their Impact on the Mental Health of Workers*, New Perspectives in Behavioral & Health Sciences,
https://doi.org/10.1007/978-981-99-7619-5_8

8.2 Analysis on Mental Health of Workers with Respect to Gender and Work Type

Gender responsive treatment takes into account the various experiences that people have in relation to gender equality and mental health. When examining the underlying causes and external pressures, culturally competent care responds to a teen or young adult's gender identification and takes that cultural component into account. This is partly due to harmful misconceptions about sexuality and body image.

Workforces with equal gender representation perform better in a variety of ways. A more unified and effective team is one of the major benefits of greater gender equality in the workplace. Diversity of thought leads to a more comprehensive approach and, as a result, a more outstanding accomplishment.

Detels et al. (2011) have written that depression will be the most important mental risk by 2030. As per WHO (2001), depression is the most observed mental stress. McDaid et al. (2005) have explained that early retirement, absenteeism in work, etc. are the main cause of depression. Cook and Glass (2014) and Acker (2006) have written that the main cause of depression among male managers in an organization is due to the increase in the number of female managers. Connell (2012) has described changes in psychological characteristics and behaviour varies with respect to sex (gender) and biological differences.

Hence to study mental stress with respect to gender and work type, the Holmes and Rahe Stress Scale is tested for 142 collected data from 71 male and 71 female of age between 25 and 50 of different professions of different countries. Tables 8.1 and 8.2 show the number of men and women who were selected for the psychometric test. Table 8.3 shows the Holmes and Rahe Stress Scale is used for testing the stress level of 142 people irrespective of gender and work type. Tables 8.4 and 8.5 show the Holmes and Rahe Stress Scale for women and men, respectively. From Tables 8.4 and 8.5, it is revealed that industrial workers, both men and women, are in high stress.

Table 8.1 Female respondents

Sl. no	Profession	Age	No. of person contacted	Place
1	Home-maker	25–50	12	India, Mexico, Bangladesh
2	Software professional	25–50	14	India, USA, New Jersey, Kannada, Mexico
3	Academician/research scholars	25–50	29	India, Mexico, China, Korea, USA
4	Industrial workers	25–50	16	India, Bangladesh, Mexico

Table 8.2 Male respondents

Sl. no	Profession	Age	No. of person contacted	Place
1	Unemployed (married and unmarried)	25–50	14	India, Mexico, Bangladesh
2	Software professional	25–50	17	India, New Jersey, Kannada, Mexico
3	Academician/research scholars	25–50	22	India, Mexico, China, Korea, USA
4	Industrial workers	25–50	18	India, Bangladesh, Mexico

The stress scale is calculated, and the average scale lies below 150 or less is called no stress/less stress, 150–300 (for 2 years) medium stress, and stress score point of more than 300 (for two years) is called as high stress.

When the same Perceived Stress Scale (PSS) is used to find a stress level of 142 persons.

According to Cohen and Williamson (1988), there are connections between PSS and measures of stress, self-reported health, health services, health behaviour, smoking status, and helping behaviour. To calculate PSS scores, responses to the four affirmatively expressed items (items 4, 5, 7, and 8) are reversed (e.g. 0 = 4, 1 = 3, 2 = 2, 3 = 1, and 4 = 0), and the sum of all scale items is then applied. Questions 2, 4, 5, and 10 of the PSS 10 item scale can be combined to create a short 4 item scale. A PSS score can be between 0 and 40, with higher numbers indicating more perceived stress. Scores between 0 and 13 are regarded as low stress. Scores between 14 and 26 would be regarded as moderate stress.

Tables 8.7 and 8.8 also show that industrial workers were under maximum stress as per PSS scores, and the result matches with Holmes and Rahe Stress Scale.

Table 8.3 Holmes and Rahe stress scale

Question	Yes	No
Loss of a spouse		
Divorce		
Separation from the spouse		
Detention in a facility such as a prison		
Death of a close relative		
A serious disease or damage		
Marriage		
Fired from a job reconciling with a spouse		
Retirement		
A family member's health or behaviour has significantly changed		
Pregnancy		
Sexual challenges		
Acquiring a new family member (by way of birth, adoption, an elderly relative moving in, etc.)		
Major business reorganization, such as a merger or bankruptcy		
Significant change in financial situation		
A close friend passed away		
Switch to a different profession		
Significant shift in the frequency of disputes with the spouse		
Obtaining a loan or mortgage to pay for a large buy foreclosure on a loan or mortgage		
Significant shift in employment responsibilities		
Son or daughter moving away (e.g. getting married or going to college)		
Issues with the in-laws		
Exceptional personal accomplishment		
Beginning or ending of a spouse's employment outside the family		
Starting or finishing formal education		
Significant shift in habitation		
Review of personal habits (including affiliations, attire, and manners)		
Issues with the boss		
Significant adjustment to labour conditions or hours		
Change of address		
Transition to a new school		
Major variation in the typical style and/or quantity of recreation		
Activities at church have changed significantly (either more or less than normal)		
A significant shift in social activities (clubs, dancing, films, and visits)		
Borrowing money to make a smaller purchase (such as a car, TV, freezer)		

(continued)

Table 8.3 (continued)

Question	Yes	No
Significant shift in sleeping patterns		
Significant shift in the frequency of family gatherings		
Significant shift in eating habits		
Christmastime vacation		
Minor legal infractions (such as traffic tickets, etc.)		

Table 8.4 Stress score for women

Sl. no	Profession	Age	Average score
1	Home-maker	25–50	432
2	Software professional	25–50	1112
3	Academician/research scholars	25–50	738
4	Industrial workers	25–50	1423

Table 8.5 Stress score for men

Sl. no	Profession	Age	Average score
1	Unemployed (married and unmarried)	25–50	1276
2	Software professional	25–50	1103
3	Academician/research scholars	25–50	378
4	Industrial workers	25–50	1335

Table 8.6 PSS psychological test

PSS question	0	1	2	3	4
How many times in the past month have you been disappointed by an unexpected event?					
How many times over the past month have you felt powerless to influence the significant events in your life?					
How often did you feel anxious and "stressed" in the past month?					
How many times in the past month did you feel assured in your capacity to deal with your personal issues?					
How frequently did it feel like things were going your way over the past month?					
How frequently did you feel like you could not handle everything you had to do in the past month					
How many times in the past month were you able to restrain annoyances in your life					
How often did you feel in control of things in the past month					
How many times in the past month have you become enraged over circumstances that were out of your control					
How many times in the past month did you feel that your problems were getting out of control					

Table 8.7 PSS score for women

Sl. no	Profession	Age	Average score
1	Home-maker	25–50	11
2	Software professional	25–50	24
3	Academician/research scholars	25–50	17
4	Industrial workers	25–50	33

Table 8.8 PSS score for men

Sl. no	Profession	Age	Average score
1	Unemployed (married and unmarried)	25–50	13
2	Software professional	25–50	18
3	Academician/research scholars	25–50	26
4	Industrial workers	25–50	38

8.3 Conclusion

It is a fact that both men and women were under high stress. The stress may be due to work or personal issues. Due to work pressure, physical illness, pressure, conflicts at workplace, financial pressure, etc. were the common causes of stress. Sometimes stress is a timely factor. It occurs due to work pressure for some time. In some cases, work pressure decreases with time. Hence, with proper counselling and medication, this type of stress can be cured.

References

Acker, J. (2006). Inequality regimes: Gender, class, and race in organizations. *Gender and Society, 20*(4), 441–464. https://doi.org/10.1177/0891243206289499

Cohen, S., & Williamson, G. (1988). Perceived stress in a probability sample of the United States. In S. Spacapan, & S. Oskamp (Eds.), *The social psychology of health*. Sage.

Connell, R. (2012). Gender, health and theory: Conceptualizing the issue, in local and world perspective. *Social Science and Medicine, 74*(11), 1675–1683.

Cook, A., & Glass, C. (2014). Above the glass ceiling: When are women and racial/ethnic minorities promoted to CEO? *Strategic Management Journal, 35*(7), 1080–1089.

Detels, R., Beaglehole, R., Lansang, M. A., & Gulliford, M. (2011). *Oxford textbook of public health*. Oxford University Press.

McDaid, D., Curran, C., & Knapp, M. (2005). Promoting mental well-being in the workplace: A European policy perspective. *International Review of Psychiatry, 17*(5), 365–373.

WHO. (2001). *The World Health Report 2001: Mental health: New understanding, new hope*. World Health Organization (WHO).

Index

S. Satapathy et al., *Occupational Health Safety Factors and Their Impact on the Mental Health of Workers*, New Perspectives in Behavioral & Health Sciences,
https://doi.org/10.1007/978-981-99-7619-5

SPRINGER NATURE

GPSR Compliance

The European Union's (EU) General Product Safety Regulation (GPSR) is a set of rules that requires consumer products to be safe and our obligations to ensure this.

If you have any concerns about our products, you can contact us on ProductSafety@springernature.com

In case Publisher is established outside the EU, the EU authorized representative is:

Springer Nature Customer Service Center GmbH
Europaplatz 3
69115 Heidelberg, Germany

The manufacturer's authorised representative in the EU is Springer Nature Customer Service Centre GmbH, Europaplatz 3, 69115 Heidelberg, Germany. If you have any concerns regarding our products, please contact ProductSafety@springernature.com

Printed and bound by CPI Group (UK) Ltd, Croydon, CR0 4YY
01/10/2026
02226300-0004